"China's phenomenal rise as a major power centre in global geopolitics under the shadow of its closed-door Communist system presents unique strategic assessment challenges for analysts and foreign affairs specialists. As a starting point, the book 'China: An Enigma' provides unique insights into China's history and its role in shaping some of its actions—past and present. For the serious student of China's contemporary studies, a must read."

—Air Chief Mshl NAK Browne, PVSM AVSM VM
Former Chief of Air Staff

"China has been in the news for some time, for some reason or the other. The voices against 'China seem to be reaching a crescendo post-COVID-19, making the timing and the title of this book absolutely apt. China, although much has been written about it, continues to remain an enigma. The author has made a commendable effort to explain China's actions, and the reasons for its behaviour. I strongly recommend the book for all China-watchers.'"

—Air Mshl KK Nohwar, PVSM VM
Former Vice Chief of Air Staff and Former DG CAPS

"China is obsessed with history. The effects of ancient history on all its present actions, or its desire to be the 'number one' in the world order, to avenge the 'century of humiliation' has been highlighted in the book. Given China's opacity, it maintains 'deception, concealment and surprise' as its key elements of battle winning strategy. It is difficult to read its intentions. The book makes a detailed study on China's psyche, and its military cum strategic thinking, so important when dealing with it on all frontiers. The author has taken pains to cover all aspects of China's behaviour, both as a country and its leadership, past and present. An important read for policy makers, strategic analysts, academia, and the Armed Forces."

—Lt Gen (Dr) V K Ahluwalia, PVSM AVSM YSM VSM**
Director, Centre for Land Warfare Studies (CLAWS)
Former Army Commander, Central Command

CHINA
AN ENIGMA

AIR MARSHAL DHIRAJ KUKREJA

CHINA
AN ENIGMA

Foreword by
Air Chief Marshal VR Chaudhari PVSM AVSM VM ADC

Introduction by
Air Marshal Anil Chopra PVSM AVSM VM VSM (Retd)

KW
KNOWLEDGE WORLD

KW Publishers Pvt Ltd
New Delhi

in association with

Centre for Air Power Studies
New Delhi

Centre for Air Power Studies
P-284, Arjan Path
Subroto Park
New Delhi 110010

Tele: (91-11) 25699131

E-mail: capsnetdroff@gmail.com
website: www.capsindia.org

ISBN   978-93-91490-94-2   Hardback
ISBN   978-93-91490-21-8   ebook

Published in India by Kalpana Shukla

KW
KNOWLEDGE WORLD

KW Publishers Pvt Ltd
4676/21, First Floor, Ansari Road
Daryaganj, New Delhi 110002
Phone: +91 11 43528107
Marketing: kw@kwpub.in
Editorial: production@kwpub.in
Website: www.kwpub.in

CENTRE FOR AIR POWER STUDIES

VISION

To be an independent centre of excellence on national security contributing informed and considered research and analyses on relevant issues.

MISSION

To encourage independent and informed research and analyses on issues of relevance to national security and to create a pool of domain experts to provide considered inputs to decision-makers. Also, to foster informed public debate and opinion on relevant issues and to engage with other think-tanks and stakeholders within India and abroad to provide an Indian perspective.

Contents

एयर चीफ मार्शल वी आर चौधरी
प वि से मे अ वि से मे वा से मे ए डी सी

Air Chief Marshal VR Chaudhari
PVSM AVSM VM ADC

Tel : (011) Off : 23012517
         Res : 23017300
         Fax : 23018853

वायु सेना मुख्यालय
नई दिल्ली - 110011
Air Headquarters
New Delhi - 110011

FOREWORD

1.   Over the years, much has been written about the growth of China and what it means for the rest of the world. Views of various think-tanks, commentators, strategists and analysts predict wide spectrum outcomes of Chinese rise. It is evident that irrespective of these assessments, China's progress is real and needs to be accommodated in all discussions on world affairs.

2.   China has made rapid economic progress over the last few decades. It has improved its infrastructure and uplifted its peoples' per capita income. Such broad based growth in Chinese potential has caused disruptions on the world stage. Chinese industrial methods have challenged conventional techniques and seen businesses flow from countries across the world into the Chinese domain. Through control, support and supervision of its industry, China has been able to capture markets globally. However, China's one child policy is beginning to affect its demographic balance, leaving it with a largely aging population and probable shortage of working manpower. Similarly, signs of stagnation in industrial output are visible in the form of underutilisation of capacities. This was most evident during the Covid pandemic which saw slowdown in trade activity and reduced outflow of industries from China. While the full impact of Covid pandemic is yet to be seen, it is apparent that the established economic systems will be re-assessed and modified to adapt to the new normal.

3.   China's economic heft has enabled its military modernisation, defence production and space exploration. While its space capabilities have catered to domestic requirements, the defence industry has been open to global defence markets. Armed with economic strength and growing military prowess, China is on course to expand its

2

footprint across the globe. However, in spite of engagements at the world stage, China has largely remained enigmatic. Chinese leadership has guarded the state's intent through strict control over the media and cyber domain. In the midst of China's growing clout, its disputes in South China Sea and border issues with some of its neighbours remain unresolved. The book dedicates a chapter to India-China relations detailing its history with a fresh perspective. Geo-strategic enthusiasts, studying regional dynamics shall find the narrative highly informative.

4. The cultural and economic heritage of China is well documented and is reflected in its stated belief of being the world's 'middle kingdom'. The country aims to regain its stature in the spheres of economic, culture and exploratory activity through relentless efforts and capability build up. The author has provided a detailed account of Chinese history, teachings in Confucianism and China's foreign policy which will help readers understand the societal and cultural rationale behind Chinese thoughts.

5. The author, Air Marshal Dhiraj Kukreja, has interest in geopolitics, defence and diplomacy, and has been writing on these topics quite frequently for the last decade plus. This project, through the Centre for Air Power Studies, is apt for the current times and should be read by students and officers, who, although know about China's growth, but may not be fully aware of the 'why' and 'how' of the growth.

Air Chief Marshal
Chief of the Air Staff

22 Nov 21

Introduction

The People's Republic of China—PRC—or simply, China—represents the most serious global threat of the 21st century. The reasons are plentiful and varied. The world leadership has been viewing China's growth for the last three to four decades, and been gullible enough to swallow the sweet talk of the Chinese leadership that its growth, be it economic or military, was peaceful. The Chinese leadership was only 'hiding its capabilities and biding its time', while the world was hoping that the Chinese economic growth would encourage China to become a more vibrant nation, imbibe some form of democracy, and open its doors to liberal Western ideas and values.

Historically, the Chinese have lived with the "Great Wall" syndrome. They chose to build a series of fortifications on the country's borders as protection against invaders. They lived with a sense of insecurity, and with a need to cut off from the outside world. Later, the industrial revolution brought the Europeans to China's shores and the seas around. Another factor that played on the Chinese psyche was the relations with Japan. Once Japan chose to adopt an active process of Europeanisation in the 19th century, it began viewing China as an antiquated civilisation, unable to defend itself against the Western forces. The First Sino-Japanese War (July 25, 1894-April 17, 1895) clearly went in favour of Japan. Emboldened by its maritime and aviation strength, Japan took on China again in the Second Sino-Japanese War (1937-1945). Finally, China got support from the Soviet Union and United States. In the end, Japan surrendered. Ever since, China has realised the need for becoming a strong military power.

The Communists under Mao Zedong used a somewhat bloody revolution to come to power. Mao coined the phrase "power flows from the barrel of the gun", which has been the Chinese approach to its regional and world affairs.

They worked to strengthen the People's Liberation Army (PLA). They also realised early that the one who controls aerospace, controls the planet. Due to the complex interplay of China's relations with the Soviet Union and USA, they also realised that to become a global power, it is important to become an economic power first.

China has had serious boundary disputes with nearly all of its 14 neighbours. With many of them, it has engaged in conflict. China also has an unfinished agenda of reunifying Taiwan which it considers as a renegade province. The serious island disputes and China's selective historic claims over islands in the East and South China Seas resulted in China realising the importance of and building, maritime and air power. It also started creating artificial islands to extend its maritime zone.

The prime objectives of China continued to be the protection of its sovereignty, recovery of lost territory, reunification of territories lost through unequal treaties, while modernising and technologically developing the country. What was not spelt out was the avenging of the 'century of humiliation', claiming new waters/islands in the Pacific Ocean with their riches both above and below the surface; and the new interest in the maritime domain. This led to a slow but stealthy transformation in the mindset of the leadership, who worked towards achieving this aim. This was being done silently. "Hide your strength, bide your time" was the guiding philosophy of Deng Xiaoping's foreign policy. He adopted the advice of Sun Tzu, China's ancient master strategist, "appear weak when you are strong, and strong when you are weak." However, when Xi Jinping assumed the post of general secretary of the Chinese Communist Party in 2012 and as president of the country in 2013, he chose to be more aggressive, and announced the arrival of China on the world stage. He also began acting to achieve China's objectives.

The task of making sense of China's aspirations has been compounded as the world moved into the 21st century, and in the recent years since Xi Jinping took over the reins. Further, he does not seem to be ready as yet, to hand over the nation to any successor. During his tenure, thus far, China has seen some significant changes in the political system, new laws and regulations being implemented—at an amazingly fast pace—some of which have upturned the existing political and economic approach and status. While Xi Jinping has encouraged globalisation, he has restricted the free flow of capital, ideas, goods, and information. Even within China, major entrepreneurs have been restricted in the conduct of their businesses and their movements curbed! Xi has used an anti-corruption drive to rein in political opposition and bring the rich entrepreneurs within his own and the Communist Party's fold.

The spread of the COVID-19 virus pandemic has played its own dynamics. Did it originate from the Wuhan laboratories or the Wuhan wet market or from some other source? Did China intentionally delay informing the World Health Organisation (WHO) and other nations of the severity of its spread when it was first detected in 2019? Xi Jinping had confined himself to within the close vicinity of Beijing. Only much later, he made a historic visit to Tibet, the first by a Chinese president in 30 years. It is now almost two years since he has physically met any world leader. Yet China is going ahead with the Winter Olympics and that may be the occasion to meet at least some global leaders such as President Putin of Russia. The sudden and rapid rise of China and the frequent global geopolitical changes make it difficult to write a book on China that does not get overtaken by events. China's aggressive forays into eastern Ladakh, the infrastructure build up in Tibet and Xinjiang, the hurried US withdrawal from Afghanistan and the resurgence of the radical Taliban, the strengthening of the Quad and the formation of the new groupings like AUKUS (Australia, United Kingdom and United States), are just a few geopolitical tremors that have directly affected China. This book is an effort to make an assessment of why China does what it does. The author, Air Marshal Dhiraj Kukreja, has years of experience in important military assignments. He has covered the entire canvass from China's ancient history, evolution and rise in the last century, and, in particular, he has covered the global approach of the current authoritative leadership of Xi Jinping. The book should make good reading for China watchers.

New Delhi   Air Marshal **Anil Chopra**
                                                              Director General
                                                                        CAPS

Acknowledgements

No project can be achieved singularly. It has to be a team effort, or a joint effort, whether the team has been formally formed or an unannounced one. My team has been unannounced, and some of the members may not even have realised their contribution towards the culmination of this project.

For the successful completion of any project, there has to be a motivating factor. I have, for long, twenty years to be precise, wanted to pen my thoughts in a book form, especially on China. Hence, first, I would like to thank China, as a nation, for being there! China has always fascinated me for its ancient history and the historical achievements therein, such as the invention of gunpowder, paper printing, fine silk and porcelain. Then came the leaders, from Mao to Xi, who have done what they have done. Yet, China continues to be an enigma!

The Centre for Air Power Studies (CAPS), both as an organisation and members, from the erstwhile Director Generals, to the present Air Marshal Anil Chopra, have in their own way encouraged me, pushed me, cajoled me, to get down to writing a book. It was just that I refused to accept their encouragements for so long! Late Air Cmde Jasjit Singh founder Director General (DG) had asked me to join CAPS in 2012, just after my superannuation. While I, informally, did join the organisation, I did not get down to writing a book. Air Mshl Vinod Patney, another former DG, encouraged me to write long articles and also entrusted me to write a chapter in a CAPS project. It was his way to get me on the path to write a book, but I did it 'my way'. Air Mshl KK Nohwar, another former DG, invited me to chair some sessions during the many seminars that CAPS conducts. It was during one such seminar that two senior Distinguished Fellows, Dr Manpreet Sethi and

Dr Shalini Chawla, extremely knowledgeable and experts in their own fields, told me separately, that while I was writing long pieces for the journals, I should also get down to some serious writing for a book. All the former and present members of CAPS, and others, who routinely presented their projects in what are known as 'Fellows Seminars', in their own way, provided the necessary push. My sincere gratitude to one and all.

And then came the first lockdown of the pandemic, and I had nowhere to go. So, I got down to writing, and then realised that I could do it, despite no physical access to any library, and enough work **at** home (emphasis intended)! Once I started writing and as I finished a chapter, another multi-talented friend, Gp Capt Ashok Chordia, came to my rescue by not just correcting my writings, but also giving me valuable suggestions on how to improve my style and content. Thank you for your help, Ashok.

I want to thank Air Marshal Anil Chopra, DG CAPS for taking the book under CAPS wings and for writing the Introduction.

My deepest gratitude to one and all, especially Ms Kalpana Shukla and her team at KW Publishers for providing assistance and bringing to my attention details that I had missed, or did not even know about. Any errors that are present in the final form are, of course, mine.

I am indeed indebted to the Chief of the Air Staff, Air Chief Marshal VR Chaudhari, to spare some time from his extremely busy schedule to write the foreword. It was indeed an encouraging gesture on his part. Thank you Chief.

Last, but not the least, I would like to thank my family, for their silent support: Neerja, my wife, who, all through the lockdown due to the pandemic, constantly reminded me of what really are the priorities in life; Nitin and Deeksha with their spouses, Kanchan and Vikram, sitting far away in Mumbai, spoke words of encouragement, over long-distance calls, during periods of loneliness and despair.

Air Marshal **Dhiraj Kukreja**
Veteran
Distinguished Fellow, CAPS

1. Understanding China

Introduction

China's rise on the global stage has been accompanied by an explosion of news and information about the country, most of which is in the 'official' Chinese media and, hence, not all of which is necessarily factual. We are told about its ageing population, its shortage of working hands due to the misplaced one-child policy, the 'bull and bear runs' in the stock market, and the investments in Africa, South America, not just in terms of money in aid, but also in strategic terms through the setting up of military bases. We can learn about the air quality in Chinese cities on the internet, which can also be used to monitor China's actions in the East and South China Seas— which some also refer to as the sea in the South of China! In many respects, it is good to learn about China, for it is one of the growing powers of the world, with many a global aspiration; from the boom or bust in trade in commodities, to its role in controlling, or contributing to global warming, the actions and choices of the Chinese leadership matter not only for themselves, but have repercussions for the world too.

Yet, as aforementioned, the information is often either inconsistent, incomplete, or inaccurate, leading to wrong conclusions or miscalculations of a response by other nations. On one day, the world can read about China pushing to establish the rule of law, and the next day, about it arresting over 300 lawyers and activists without following the legal norms and due processes.[1] In the latter half of 2015, Chinese officials admitted to having wrongly estimated the country's consumption of coal by as much as 17 per cent; this news immediately raised questions about its commitment towards a safe climate and accomplishments that it has claimed in energy efficiency and greenhouse gas emissions! Dramatic and misleading headlines in its government-owned media, while highlighting its achievements, leave the other nations of the world perplexed about their authenticity.

The challenge of trying to understand China has been compounded manifold with the election of Xi Jinping as the general secretary of the Chinese Communist Party (CCP) in November 2012 followed by his election to the president's post in early 2013; his methodical purging of any opposition to his policies, by friend and foe alike, in the CCP, has led to an unprecedented centralisation of power. It is only now that answers to questions about his intentions are unravelling: he has shown himself to be a strong nationalist who wants to place China in its perceived rightful place in the world order as against USA, with reforms within the country's politics, economy, and more importantly, foreign policy. Nevertheless, to understand China, as to what it is today, and why it is doing what it is doing, one needs to take a brief look into Chinese history. While even ancient Chinese history has been continually affecting the behaviour of the country, at this stage, only what is relevant, along with history from the Mao era, is being mentioned, not necessarily in a sequential order, and interspersed with current happenings.

Chinese History

Four-character *chengyu*, or idioms, are typical of the Mandarin language. They, generally, contain some nuggets of wisdom or a tale of morality from ancient Chinese narrations of myths or historical events. Chinese leaders often make use of *chengyu* to inject some life into their dull and monotonous policy announcements; this practice of quoting from the ancient texts has been followed by successive Chinese leaders, throughout the 1990s and into the 2000s. Former Chinese leader Deng Xiaoping, popularised the maxim *taoguang yanghui*—"hide one's capacities and bide one's time"—in the early 1990s to summarise China's foreign policy; he also embedded this phrase in a much longer 24-character expression, which translates into a well-planned course of action: "Observe the situation calmly. Stand firm in our positions. Respond cautiously. Conceal own capabilities and await an opportune moment. Never claim leadership. Take some action". There are a number of interpretations, but the one most intriguing is that of Yang Wenchang, former vice minister of foreign affairs in an op-ed from *China*

Daily titled "Diplomatic Words of Wisdom" wherein not only are the origins of the idiom's roots mentioned, but also an explanation of how it seemed to be at odds with the then foreign policy[2]. In 2009, President Hu Jintao amended the last eight characters to "uphold (*jianchi*) keeping a low profile and actively (*jiji*) achieve something (*taoguang yanghui, yousuo zuowei*)".[3] Since then, China has left out these reserved and unassuming references and today, speaks of acting its role and undertaking its responsibilities on the global stage.

The intricacy and indistinctness of the Chinese language in trying to appreciate what is *shi*, is supplemental. The actual meaning of a word often depends on the tone, context and intent. *Shi* is one such word, which cannot be directly translated into English, and, hence, leads to misinterpretations; yet, *shi* is the core of China's strategy! The concept, if it can be termed so, thus, can be best described as 'an alignment of forces', for a skilled strategist to exploit, to ensure victory over a superior opponent.[4] *Shi*, as per Sun Tzu's *The Art of War*, can be used by a knowledgeable strategist to turn events to his will and get enemies to act in ways for further gains. Almost all Chinese leaders in the past decades have believed in, and used, *shi* at some time or the other. Mao used *shi* when he secretly approached Nixon in 1969, to offer China's support against the Soviet Union; Deng Xiaoping used *shi* in 1979 while visiting USA, initiating an economic revolution in China, funded by Western nations, but completely on China's terms and conditions (exactly as created in the mind of Sun Tzu)! The West kept helping China's rise, under the false notion that China would transform into an open and a more democratic society, but, in actuality, it has grown more autocratic, simultaneously spreading information to its people that portrays the West as a debauched society of imperialist thugs!

In his opening address, on taking over the reins as general secretary of the Communist Party in 2012, Xi Jinping, used a phrase that no other Chinese leader had ever used in public: *qiang zhongguo meng*—"strong nation dream"; such a grand announcement had never been made before the world by any Chinese leader any time earlier.[5] The "Chinese Dream" is now an official goal, with a timeline of 2049, the centenary of Mao's takeover, when China will become "a fully developed nation". In November 2014, Xi spelt out his vision for the nation's future foreign policy to the country's diplomatic and military elite, by stating *daguo waijio*—"big country diplomacy"; this was followed, a month later, in his address to the Politburo, that he intended to "make China's voice heard again, and inject more Chinese elements into international rules".[6] The fulfilment of this dream could also actually imply supremacy in the world in all domains, economic, military, and cultural. Xi obviously opines that his usage of *shi* is favourable.

Chinese leaders have drawn their strategies not just from their ancient texts, such as those of Sun Tzu, but also from history, especially the era of the Warring States, a period of two-and-a-half centuries that began around 475 BCE and ended with unification under the Qin Dynasty in 221 BCE. There is a reason for it; of the seven military classics of China, four were written during this period, including Sun Tzu's *The Art of War*.[7] Apart from the era being one of intense warfare, it also brought in bureaucratic and military reforms with complex bureaucracies and centralised governments becoming a norm, which to a certain extent is being followed even today.[8]

The nucleus of all the victorious strategies harvested from that period is deception, which the Chinese have always considered as the most essential feature of their approach. Chinese history is replete with stories of their most celebrated military victories that are based on deception; cunningness in their heroes is an extremely common trait and mentioned in their narratives. Chinese literature often highlights the role of deception and the need for a sage, a 'wise man', who can penetrate through the fog of deception all around to find the reality. Michael Pillsbury, a leading American China expert, who has spent most of his life studying China and working as an adviser to US governments, intelligence agencies and think-tanks, and also a China-adviser to President Trump, sums up Chinese history as, "On the outside, be benevolent; on the inside, be ruthless".[9]

Sun Tzu permeates modern Chinese strategy, influencing everything from deception to espionage. Despite having been written more than 2,500 years ago, during an age when agriculture was predominant, his writings have remained relevant through the industrial age to the present-day information age. No discussion on Chinese strategy is complete without a discussion on Sun Tzu. The Western world first 'discovered' Sun Tzu in the 18th century or thereabouts. Wilhelm II, the emperor of Germany, is reported to have said, "I wish I could have read Sun Tzu before World War I"; General Douglas

MacArthur once stated that he always kept a copy of Sun Tzu's *Art of War* on his desk[10]. Such is the influence of Sun Tzu's writings on military strategists all over the world, not just the Chinese! Specific applications of Sun Tzu occasionally are included in People's Liberation Army (PLA) literature, and are used not just by the army but also the other two arms, the People's Liberation Army Air Force (PLAAF) and People's Liberation Army Navy (PLAN). The reader can well imagine how the following, Sun Tzu's 12 methods of deception, have been received by the Chinese armed forces.

- When one is capable, give the appearance of being incapable.
- When one is active, give the appearance of being inactive.
- When one is near, give the appearance of being far.
- When one is far, give the appearance of being near.
- When one's opponents are greedy for advantage, tempt them.
- When one's opponents are in chaos, seize them.
- When one's opponents are secure, prepare for them.
- When one's opponents are strong, evade them.
- When one's opponents are angry, aggravate them.
- When one's opponents are humble, make them arrogant.
- When one's opponents are at ease, make them weary.
- When one's opponents are friendly to each other, divide them.[11]

Moving ahead from ancient history: China's one hundred years of humiliation are deeply etched in the psyche of the Chinese people, more so of the leadership. The President of China's first republic, Sun Yat-sen, described this period in a speech in 1924: "Today we are the poorest and the weakest nation in the world, and occupy the lowest position in international affairs; the rest of mankind is the carving knife and the serving dish, while we are the fish and the meat".[12] Sun Yat-sen further amplified his description of China as being worse than that of India because, "India was the favoured wife of Britain while China was the common prostitute of all the powers".[13] With the turn of the century, this desire to overcome the sense of weakness and humiliation, felt for many decades, is now included in the writings of many a present-day Chinese thinker, and propagates a historical mandate to regain China's place as a global power. The unstable history of China through the five decades spanning from the 1930s to the 1970s did not help in any way to redress Sun Yat-sen's complaint about the country's place in the world order. The goals that China has set for itself and which it is aggressively pursuing today, of regaining its rightful place in the world through the Chinese Dream, are a direct result of this description in Chinese history; the CCP contends that only it can realise and restore China's pride. As Mao declared on October 1, 1949, at Tiananmen Square, "China has stood up ... Without the CCP, there is no new China!"[14]

The desire to overcome this sense of injustice and to avenge the humiliation inflicted is not just in the thoughts of the Chinese leadership, but can also be found in the writings of many a contemporary Chinese writer and thinker during the 1990s through to the early 2000s. A well-respected scholar from the renowned Tsinghua University in Beijing, Yan Xuetong, has stated in one of his writings that China had a historical mandate to regain its place in the global order: "The rise of China is granted by nature. In the last two thousand years, China has enjoyed superpower status several times.... Even as recently as 1820, just twenty years before the Opium War, China accounted for 30 per cent of the world's GDP. This history of superpower status makes the Chinese people very proud of their country, on the one hand, and, on the other hand, very sad about China's international status. They believe China's decline to be a historical mistake, which they should correct."[15] Not all Chinese scholars and thinkers are, however, in agreement with this sort of an openly ambitious thought process and continue to favour Deng Xiaoping's lower-key process.

Pre-Xi Jinping Period

Revolutions, political and social anarchy, and disconnections in political ideologies, mess up a large period of Chinese history. Successive Chinese governments had, for long, portrayed their country as backward and, hence, in need of international assistance for its 'peaceful rise', while denying any aspirations for global leadership. As Michael Pillsbury, author of the 2015 book, *The Hundred-Year Marathon* (HYM), succinctly explains in the book, it was deception in totality! China has received financial and technological assistance for its growth, with the Western nations fooling themselves about its 'peaceful rise', while the Chinese had already been working on a

"China-led world order" to gain its 'proper' place in the world, running the 'Hundred-Year Marathon'[16].

The 'rejuvenation' narrative, as noted earlier, is well-understood and much-desired in China. Stories evoke memories of the country that was once known as the Middle Kingdom and which commanded levies from the rest of the world. China was once known as the land of innovation, creating paper, gunpowder, printing, and the compass. It was an expansive, outward-looking power during the Ming dynasty; Admiral Zheng He, from the emperor's court, sailed with a flotilla of more than 300 ships throughout Asia, to the Horn of Africa and the Red Sea, with a mandate from the emperor to collect tribute and establish ties with all rulers around the Indian Ocean.[17]

Alongside the rejuvenation narratives are also tales from history—ancient and contemporary—which are left out, but are also deeply etched in the memories of many Chinese. These relate to periods that renew remembrances that arouse feelings of dishonour and shame, such as the 'one hundred years of humiliation' (1849-1949), when China was occupied by foreign powers and experienced crushing defeats in the Opium Wars, which demeaned its standing as an ancient civilisation; some periods from the 20th century history too, play similarly on the people's minds, when they suffered extensively due to the actions of their own government during, for example, the Great Leap Forward, the Cultural Revolution, and the Tiananmen Square massacre. While the people may silently accept history as it exists, some leaders, such as Xi, seem determined to right the wrongs done to China, as it so appears.

Xi Jinping, when he took over the reins as the general secretary of the CCP on November 15, 2012, made his vision known to the people of China, and the world, at large, immediately thereafter during a press conference. He spoke about the rampant corruption within the Party and the need to ensure that the CCP served the people; the essence of his vision, however, was his call for the great revival or rejuvenation of China, while reflecting on the contribution of the country during its 5,000 years of history; he also acknowledged the contributions by earlier leaders towards the great revival, which had "failed one time after another".[18]

Xi Jinping, however, is not the first leader in recent times to use the theme of rejuvenation as a reminder to the Chinese people of the country's glorious past, in an effort to unite them in their quest towards building a modern China. Deng Xiaoping, and his successors, Jiang Zemin, and Hu Jintao, all called for the rejuvenation of the country. During the past three decades plus, the Chinese people have experienced an extraordinary period of economic and political reform, and opening up of the country to the world, a process, which the leaders thought could help reclaim its place as a global power. Seeking to realise the common vision with his predecessors, Xi, however, has been different, by largely rejecting their path of reform and opening up; instead, he has initiated reform without opening up! Not only has the current Chinese leadership adopted a process of institutional revision to reverse the many political, social, and economic changes of the past three decades plus of liberal reforms, but has also shed the low-profile foreign policy, as was advocated by Deng Xiaoping, and instead, has been adopting some bold and aggressive initiatives.

Travelling back again into history: Mao Zedong, also known as Chairman Mao, was the founder of the People's Republic of China (PRC) and the chairman of the CCP from 1949, until his death in 1976—a long quarter of a century of what is also known as the First Revolution. By 1976, the year of Mao's and his Premier, Zhou Enlai's deaths, the leadership had begun the process of recovery from the political discords, social disorder, and destitution caused by economic policies, which had become the norm during most of the 25 years of their rule. Xi Jinping, himself, had been a victim of the mal-administration of Mao. In the 1960s, Xi's father, a leading revolutionary in his own right and holding the position of vice-premier in the government, was jailed after being branded a traitor for his bourgeois background. Xi, then a fifteen-year-old youth, was despatched to a labour camp for several years where he worked in an agricultural commune. He, however, did not feel any resentment towards the Communist Party; instead, he resolved to gain its membership and after being denied many times, he was finally accepted in 1974. Xi Jinping started his rise in the CCP, alongside Zhou Enlai's programme of 1975, to revitalise China's economy and society. He was permitted to return to Beijing the same year and studied chemical engineering at Tsinghua University, infused with Mao's ideas and Marxism-Leninism.

Deng Xiaoping was the 'paramount leader' from 1978 to 1989, after a brief and bloodless power struggle when Hua Guofeng was ousted. The term 'paramount leader' needs an explanation here. In modern Chinese politics, the term paramount leader, also known as the supreme leader, is an informal term for the most prominent leader in China (the present incumbent is Xi Jinping); it is neither a formal position, nor an office by itself. The incumbent is generally the General Secretary of the CCP and chairman of the Central Military Commission (CMC). The term was very widely used during Deng's era, when he wielded tremendous political power without holding any official or government position at any given time; yet, during his tenure, he initiated major transformations in the economic and political systems, which he termed as China's Second Revolution. Mao's legacy was a highly-controlled state, characterised by very personalised and concentrated power in an organisation that employed coercive techniques. This regime of controls exercised by the state since the 1950s was eased by the early 1980s by delegation of significant economic authority to provincial and local officials. International participation was invited through Foreign Direct Investment (FDI) and trade by 1984; by the mid-1990s, the state-run enterprises, which were, until then, the foundation of the urban economy and had a monopoly in ownership and employment, were begun to be dismantled, making space for private and cooperative ventures. This, combined with encouragement to rural enterprises, resulted in a dramatic growth rate of China's Gross Domestic Product (GDP) to over 8 per cent, sustained for more than two decades, elevating millions of its citizens out of poverty, thus, gaining international acclaim.[19]

Officially, Deng Xiaoping decided to retire from the top positions in 1989, when he resigned as the chairman of the Central Military Commission, but finally took a back-seat from active politics in 1992. He was succeeded by Jiang Zemin, who had been declared as the general secretary of the Party in 1989 and president of China in 1993. Although Jiang gained firm control of the government, the policies continued under the shadow of Deng's political and economic philosophies. Jiang Zemin, along with his Premier,

Zhu Rongji, nevertheless, continued with the economic and political reforms, prominent being the inclusion of the private sector in the political system; successful business people were actively welcomed as members of the CCP, a first in China! China's looking outward towards the world also continued with it joining the World Trade Organisation (WTO) in 2001; Chinese state-owned enterprises were encouraged to seek natural resources, much needed to sustain the economic growth, from other countries, and the Chinese people were motivated to move out of the country for employment and further studies.

Alongside the economic reforms and achievements were reforms in the political sphere too. The highly personalised culture of governance was replaced with collective leadership and a more institutionalised succession process; political authority was devolved to local and provincial officials, and China began accepting international policy advice and financial assistance through approved Non-Governmental Organisations (NGOs).

Following Jiang Zemin was the era of Hu Jintao and his Premier, Wen Jiabao from 2002 to 2012. The reforms—economic, political and diplomatic—continued, with China giving assurances to its nervous neighbours, in particular, and an uneasy world, at large, that its rise was a peaceful one. China's standing in the world order, as an economic heavyweight, reached a new high in the midst of the global financial crisis of 2008. In the summer of 2008, China hosted the Olympic Games, notwithstanding the widespread global objections against its human rights record and the severe air pollution in Beijing. The conduct of the Games earned laurels internationally and consolidated the position of a rising star in the Politburo, one who oversaw the preparations, namely, Xi Jinping.

The continued strength of China's economy throughout the global financial crisis, started calls within China for it to take its rightful place in the world order to shape international norms and institutions; many senior officials in the economic and diplomatic fraternity, and the military openly stated that the long-predicted decline of USA and the rise of China, to occur some time in the 21st century, had indeed begun! China's military was a major beneficiary of its economic rise with a double-digit budget; the growth in capabilities also fuelled its assertions and the rhetoric around sovereign claims in the East and South China Seas (SCS) to transform into action. Overseeing these moves in the SCS was the same rising star, Xi Jinping.

Despite the significant economic, diplomatic and associated military successes, the decade of Hu Jintao is also called the "lost decade".[20] Conspicuous incongruities reared their heads in the domestic political and economic environment. The CCP was seen as having lost its ideological stance, and for many of its 80-odd million members, it had become just a stepping-stone for personal or political gains; corruption became a centre-stage issue throughout the Party and the country. By 2010, protests across the country increased as the economic growth slowed down; even with the economic success of the past years with the low-cost manufacturing, China did not have much to show by way of inventiveness, or the development of the services sector, the important indices of any advanced economy. Xi Jinping took over power, determined to change the trend of the downward slide.

Xi Jinping Takes Guard

As governor of Fujian province, in the year 2000, Xi Jinping, relatively unknown and not even a full member of the Central Committee of the CCP, had shared his thoughts on leadership in an interview to the Chinese journal, *Zhongua Ernu*, stating that a new leader "needed to continue working on the foundations" laid by his predecessor, while alongside "coming with his own plans and set an agenda during the first year". He equated leadership with a relay race, in which a successor has to "receive the baton properly, and then run it across the line".[21] On taking over as general secretary in 2012, during his first press conference, Xi emphasised the baton analogy, stating that the responsibility of the Party leadership is to "take over the relay baton passed on to us by history" to achieve "the great renewal of the Chinese nation".[22] Be that as it may, for all his statements in interviews, Xi, on receiving the baton, seems to be running the race quite differently from his predecessors, with a plan of his own, being executed in his own style, and at a pace of his own.

While the emphasis on corruption and an assertive stance in the South and Eastern Seas are carry-forwards from the later stages of Hu's tenure, the increased efforts have greatly altered the domestic political landscape and the country's role on the regional and global geopolitical stage. Collective leadership has been side-stepped and a dramatic centralisation of authority in Xi Jinping, under his personal leadership, has placed him on a pedestal as the 'prime leader'; the role of the CCP and the state in the society and the economy has been heightened to control the flow of ideas, culture, and capital into and out of the country; China's involvement in world affairs has sought to be elevated with the significant projection of power—soft and hard. If Deng Xiaoping called the transformative process of his time the "Second Revolution", this can be called China's "Third Revolution" with Xi Jinping, probably the most powerful leader since Mao Zedong, as the chief architect.

Xi Jinping's focus in his reforms is on the 'great revival' or rejuvenation of the nation. As aforementioned, his predecessors too had wanted to 'revive' China, but their methods were comparatively docile in comparison to those of the current leadership. Following what he had said in his interview to the Chinese journal, *Zhongua Ernu*, in 2000 (see note 21), he set his agenda and priorities immediately on taking over as the general secretary of the CCP, and then later, within a few months, as the president.

Xi's 'Third Revolution' for China has taken off with a very distinctive strategy. As the general secretary of the CCP, he has accrued more power, both institutionally and personally. Unlike his predecessors, he has placed himself at the helm of the most important committees and commissions that oversee or formulate government policies; in so far as personal power is concerned, he has demanded pledges of loyalty from military and Party leaders, sidelining those who have doubts or have questioned his policies, through the sweeping anti-corruption laws. Writing in 2000 about China's transition from the Mao era to the then leadership of Deng Xiaoping, David Shambaugh had remarked, "If one of the hallmarks of the Maoist state was the penetration of society, then the Dengist state was the withdrawal. The organisational mechanisms for the state penetration and manipulation were substantially reduced or dismantled altogether."[23] Xi and his team, on the other hand, have launched a forceful transformation to increase the role of the CCP in the political, social, and economic domains. The increase in the Party's role, in the leadership's vision, is an effort to protect China's society and economy from foreign competition and the influence of the depravity prevalent in the Western nations, through a virtual wall of regulatory, legal, and technological hurdles. The obstructions are, however, selectively placed; while there are restrictions on what flows in, the flow of ideas out of China, through the official propaganda machine of Chinese media, Confucius Institutes—government sponsored language and cultural centres—and think-tanks, is encouraged. Similarly, the Chinese government permits the outflow of capital to certain sectors, or nations where national interest is involved, but does restrict the inflow of capital where national interest, in its perception, is compromised, as is the general practice of all nations. Finally, what is very visible is the move away from the predecessors' commitment to maintain a low diplomatic profile, to one that displays China's assertiveness and desires to mould international institutions and norms as per China's wishes. Xi Jinping has established the country's first military logistics base in Djibouti, and has, through fair or foul means, taken a significant stake in strategic ports not just in Asia, but elsewhere in Europe too. Xi Jinping seems to have modelled Chinese politics and foreign policy according to his vision and belief that these would translate into his Chinese dream.

Can Xi Succeed?

Consolidation of power during his first five years in office retarded the implementation of some of Xi Jinping's reforms; this was necessitated due to factionalism within the Party, and opposition to his anti-corruption reforms by disgruntled officials.[24] Nevertheless, with the passage of time, with the Jiang Zemin faction silenced, and the opposition snuffed out through the implementation of strict ant-corruption laws, an understanding, and a reluctant acceptance, of his reforms soon emerged.[25]

The world sees China as more assertive under Xi. But, as far as the Chinese government is concerned, it still insists on calling it a peaceful development strategy. The Party, however, has modified it with an open responsibility, taking a very strong stand over the territorial integrity of the country and preserving its right to decide what is best for the country. The Chinese leadership is well aware of the uneasiness that many nations feel about China's growth; as an assurance of its peaceful intentions, China has been promoting the concept that all can be winners. It also emphasises on mutually beneficial international collaboration, to facilitate an increased involvement in world affairs, but all under the guidance of China. This is the motive behind its policy to promote mutual interest, shared responsibilities, and a shared partaking in international affairs!

Central to Xi's vision of a rejuvenated nation is a China that sits at the epicentre of Asia and beyond. This approach has manifested itself in the advocating of a new kind of great-power relationship, with 'the maritime silk road' and 'the silk road economic belt', now popularised as the 'One Belt One Road' (OBOR) strategy, and a further shortened nomenclature of 'Belt and Road Initiative' (BRI). Howsoever it has been received by the world, these are policies designed to showcase benefits for both China and its partners as a win-win situation, and developing strategic partnerships with them, whether it is from its assertiveness or coercion, is a different issue. These initiatives, thus, offer several broader perceptions into the changes underway and their implications for the rest of the world.

First, Xi and his team are playing a long game. The policies for control rather than competition through opening up, in both the political and the economic domains, often lead to a fallacy of the outcomes that appear to be not so advantageous in the near term, but are often of greater strategic value within China. Xi's centralisation of power through political reforms, has given him more decision-making authority, but has also led to policy-paralysis at the local levels, which, in turn, has led to a lower growth of the economy. The leadership is, however, not too perturbed about it, as with its authority, it encourages even loss-making State-Owned Enterprises (SOEs) to make strategic investments in high-risk economies outside the country, through the BRI.

Second, centralisation of power and the increasing control over information outflow, makes it challenging for the outside world, and even the local populace at times, to assess the degree of consensus of the leader's decisions and the direction that they are meant to take. May be not as forceful as in the pre-Xi era, but discussions on the government's current policies do continue amongst the scholars and officials. A reduced inflow of FDI has been attributed to the methodology of the anti-corruption drive; Xi's very own pet-project of the BRI has also drawn criticism on the investments being made. These are also leading to muted opposition in parts of the upper echelons of the CCP.

Third, Xi's personal desire of making China great again has caused an overlap between the interests of China and the rest of the world, creating challenges and opportunities for alliances. While Chinese initiatives in the BRI and the Asian Infrastructure Investment Bank (AIIB) offers investment opportunities to Chinese businesses, China's rhetoric on its commitment to globalisation and claim to international leadership, is open to confrontation by the rest of the world. Simultaneously, China's growing ambition is setting the stage for conflicts, both economically and operationally; the trade war with USA and regional confrontations with Taiwan, in the SCS, and with India, are examples.

Fourth, the least understood, and the greatest emerging challenge, is that of understanding the policies of dual-reform. The interpretation of China's domestic, economic and political reforms is, today, of great importance to the rest of the world, as never before. There was a time in the not so recent past, when China's human rights record was largely ignored by the world as its internal issue, mainly due to trade interests, but is today being questioned! What China practises for itself in other nations, such as the spread of Chinese culture and political values, through foreign media and the network of Confucius Institutes, is not allowed to be reciprocated within China; similarly, investments by SOEs in mines, ports, oilfields and other strategic infrastructure in countries, is not permitted by foreign companies within China. China appears to be following in the footsteps of powers like USA, USSR and UK that, too, in the past, followed partisan policies seeking leadership of an accommodative world, wanting to exploit others to protect and further their own interests!

The reader may well wonder if Xi's 'Third Revolution' has the sustaining power with such assertive, restrictive and parochial policies? So far, there is no real evidence of any major domestic reversal. The results of the 19th Party Congress held in October 2017 suggest that Xi has only strengthened his position in the CCP, and with it, the mandate for reforms. The tenets of socialism, as practised in China, have been included in the Constitution as "Xi Jinping Thought on Socialism with Chinese Characteristics for a New Era" (abbreviated as Xi Jinping Thought), in a manner that was earlier accorded only to Mao. The 25-year-old tradition of naming a successor for the post of general secretary was not followed by Xi, leading to speculation that he would be elected once again in 2022, when he should actually be relinquishing the post. The top positions of the CCP have been filled by Xi with his supporters; while in the Politburo, 18 of the 25 members are Xi's allies, the Politburo Standing Committee (PBSC) has 4 of the 7, not including Xi himself.[26] The CCP in its four-day plenary session that concluded on October 29, 2020, gave its stamp of approval for the 14th Five-Year Plan (2021-2025) for 'National Economic and Social Development and the Long-Range Objectives Through the Year 2035'. This probably is a strong indicator that Xi Jinping essentially intends to be at the helm to lead China through this period.

The spread of the pandemic, both within China and the entire world, of the 'Wuhan virus' in 2020—a term disliked and rejected by Xi—has affected the growth and spread of the Chinese model, more so Xi's pet project of the BRI. Even while China's economy, supposedly, is showing trends of growth, international companies, with the open support of their parent nations, have begun to make plans to move out of China; countries like Japan, Vietnam, and India are promising them incentives to relocate. The military might of China's PLA is also being tested by its own provocative behaviour against India, Taiwan, and in the Eastern and Southern Seas, challenging Xi's dream of a resurgent China at the pinnacle of the global pecking order.

Foretelling the future is quite often an exercise in futility. Thinking about China's future, if its modern history is any guide, is an exercise in frustration. No major country has undergone as many sweeping and pervasive changes in policies as the People's Republic of China has since its founding in 1949. Nevertheless, a number of factors had pointed towards greater continuity in the future, that is, until the pandemic struck in early 2020 and disrupted Xi's plans.

Whether Xi Jinping will succeed or not, only history will tell!

Notes

1. Elizabeth C. Economy, *The Third Revolution* (Oxford University Press, 2018), p. 46.

2. Yang Wenchang, "Diplomatic Words of Wisdom", op-ed *China Daily*, October 29, 2011, available on www.chinadaily.com.cn, accessed on October 6, 2020.

3. Shivshankar Menon, "What China's Rise Means for the World", January 2, 2016, https://thewire.in/external-affairs/what-chinas-rise-means-for-the-world, accessed on October 6, 2020.

4. Sandipan Deb, "China's 100-year Marathon to Rule the World and Reshape It", *Opinion- The Mint*, October 20, 2019, Opinion (livemint.com), accessed on August 10, 2020.

5. Ibid.

6. Ibid.

7. "Seven Military Classics", Wikipedia, https://en.wikipedia.org/wiki/Seven_ Military_Classics#:~:text=The%20Seven%20Military%20Classics%20 %28traditional%20Chinese%3A%20%E6%AD%A6%E7%B6%93%E4%B8%83% E6%9B%B8%3B%20simplified,which%20also%20included%20Sun-tzu%27s%20 The%20Art%20of%20War, accessed on August 12, 2020.

8. Ibid.

9. Deb, n. 4.

10. Fumio Ota, "Sun Tzu in Contemporary Chinese Strategy", *Joint Force Quarterly* 73, 2nd Quarter, April 2014, available online, www.ndupress.ndu.edu, accessed on October 14, 2020.

11. Commander Mark Metcalf, USN, "Deception is the Chinese Way of War", *USNI Journal*, Vol 143/2/1/1368, February 2017, available online at https://www.usni.org/ magazines/proceedings/2017/february/deception-chinese-way-war, accessed on October 14, 2020.

12. Orville Schell and John Delury, "Wealth and Power: China's Long March to the 21st Century", Chapter 6, "A Sheet of Loose Sand: Sun Yat-sen, 1866-1925"; Quote attributed to Sun Yat-sen, China's first president, from a speech he made in 1924; available in his online biography, www.sites.asiasociety.org, accessed on October 6, 2020.

13. Menon, n. 3.

14. Ibid.

15. Yan Xuetong, "The Rise of China in Chinese Eyes", *Journal of Contemporary China*, Vol 10, Issue 26, 2001, published online on August 2, 2010, https://www.tandfonline. com/doi/abs/10.1080/10670560123407, accessed on October 17, 2020.

16. Deb, n. 4.

17. Kallie Szczepanski, "Biography of Zheng He, Chinese Admiral", https://www. thoughtco.com/zheng-he-ming-chinas-great-admiral-195236#:~:text=Zheng%20

He%20%281371%E2%80%931433%20or%201435%29%20was%20a%20
Chinese,met%20up%20with%20the%20admiral%27s%20huge%20Chinese%20
fleet, accessed on September 24, 2020.

18. "Full Text of Xi's Address to the Media", *China Daily*, November 16, 2012, http://
www.chinadaily.com.cn/china/2012cpc/2012-11/16/content_15934514.htm,
accessed on September 10, 2020.

19. Economy, n. 1.

20. Ibid.

21. Xiaohuai Yang, "Xi Jinping: My Road into Politics", *Zhongua Ernu*, Interview from
the summer of 2000 in the Chinese journal, translated by Carsten Boyer Thogersen
and Susanne Posborg of Nordic Institute of Asian Studies, available on https://
www.asiaportal.info/xi-jinping-my-road-into-politics/, accessed on October 17,
2020.

22. "Xi Leads Top Leadership, Meeting Press", Xinhua, November 15, 2012,
(china-embassy.org), accessed on October 17, 2020.

23. David Shambaugh, "The Chinese State in the Post-Mao Era", in David Shambaugh,
ed., *The Modern Chinese State* (Cambridge University Press), online publication in
October 2009, summary available on https://www.cambridge.org/core/books/
modern-chinese-state/chinese-state-in-the-postmao-era/4BA33FE4C5E59912B
23BA6974AD576F3, accessed on October 19, 2020.

24. Keira Lu Huang, "Xi Jinping's Reforms Encounter 'Unimaginably Fierce Resistance',
Chinese State Media Says in 'Furious' Commentary," *South China Morning Post*,
August 21, 2015, (scmp.com), accessed on October 30, 2020.

25. Tara Francis Chan, "Factional Warring and Failed 'Coups' May be the Reason XI
Jinping Wants to Rule China Forever", *Business Insider*, March 12, 2018, accessed on
October 30, 2020.

26. Minxin Pei, "China's Return to Strongman Rule", *Foreign Affairs*, November 1,
2017, https://www.foreignaffairs.com/articles/china/2017-11-01/chinas-return-
strongman-rule, accessed on October 19, 2020.

2.   China: A Lesson in History

Chinese History: A Starter

Very few countries in the world can boast of an ancient civilisation as China's with a long history of almost 5,000 years, which is, at times, puzzling, but deep and profound. As is with other ancient civilisations of the world, the Chinese way of life and its culture can be traced to a fusion of small original tribes, which developed till they became the country of today. A study of the long history of China shows that its people have contributed much to the advancement of not just the country, and to the amelioration of its history, but also to the development of the world at large. History is glorified in China. At every opportunity, ordinary people speak about their 5,000 years of culture: *wuqiannian de wenhua*.[1] And for the government, it is the benchmark for legitimacy in the present. But it is also a beast that lurks in the shadows.

Chinese society has progressed through five major stages—Primitive Society, Slave Society, Feudal Society, Semi-feudal and Semi-colonial Society—to reach the Socialist Society, as we see it today. Chinese history is replete with the rise and fall of dynasties almost from the beginning, with the Mandate of Heaven, as believed by the people, given to the rulers to be their emperors. On a dynasty losing power, it was also meant that it had lost the Mandate of Heaven.[2]

Readers may wonder as to why is it necessary to learn about ancient China. Ancient Chinese history has influenced modern China in a manner that today when one studies Chinese society, or its economy, or military doctrines, or even about Chinese 'informatics', there is a legacy that has influenced modern China. Additionally, ancient China is known for a rich culture, prevalent not just in modern China, but all over the world. From small farming communities rose dynasties such as the Zhou Dynasty (1046-256 BCE), Qin Dynasty (221-206 BCE), and Ming dynasty (1368-1644 CE), each contributing in its own way to the region. During the Zhou Dynasty, for example, the script for writing was standardised and working with iron was honed; famous thinkers like Confucius and Sun Tzu lived during this period and shared their philosophies, which are prevalent till today.[3]

Confucianism, Taoism, and Buddhism were the three main beliefs and religions of ancient China, which have individually and collectively influenced ancient and modern Chinese society. Values and ideas from the three religions continue to influence modern Chinese culture, albeit in small pockets. Despite the differences and occasional contradictions in the philosophies of the three religions, the ancient Chinese society held each of them in high regard and absorbed the diverse teachings into its different areas of life. These religions are widespread, even today, in the regions surrounding China, in East and Southeast Asia, India, and also in a few Western nations.

Ancient China

China has given to the world, the oldest existing culture. The name 'China' comes from the Sanskrit word 'Cina', derived from the name of the Chinese Qin Dynasty, pronounced 'Chin'; translated as 'Cin' by the Persians, this spread through trade along the Silk Route from China to the rest of the world.[4] Although there is a Sanskrit link to the name, the country has had different nomenclatures through the centuries. The Romans and Greeks knew about China as the 'land where silk comes from' and, hence, called it 'Seres'.[5] Marco Polo, the renowned voyager, introduced Europe to China in 13th century CE and referred to it as 'Cathay', considered as a poetic name for the country![6] The Europeans knew of China for long through trade via the Silk Route, but it was not until 1516 CE that the name 'China' appeared in print in Duarte Barbosa's accounts of his travels in East Asia.[7]

As aforementioned, it has been referred to by different names, but traditionally, it has called itself *Zhonggou*, which means 'Middle Kingdom', at times translated as 'Central Kingdom' also.[8] Ethnocentrism is a belief that has a cultural or historical connotation, that one's own country is the 'centre' of the world; for example, it is only the people residing in USA, who call themselves 'Americans', even when there are over 30 other countries in North, Central and South America! Similar is the significance attributed to the term 'Middle Kingdom', which has evolved over centuries to mean differently from a geographic and political viewpoint.

Thousands of years ago, China was divided into multiple independent states before being unified under a single empire. During this period, the term Middle Kingdom referred to the existent centres of these various states. The term reflected the culturally significant regions of China that were located along the valley of the Yellow river, considered to be the cradle of Chinese civilisation.[9] In the subsequent years, when China was unified under a single emperor, the term referred to the region where the emperor resided, which changed depending upon which region the emperor belonged to. With the passage of time, right through the 19th and 20th centuries, the term Middle Kingdom has included the country as a whole, rather than a small area within, thus, giving a feeling of belongingness and solidarity to the people of China.

While it is commonly accepted that the human race originated in the African continent, the earliest traces of human inhabitation, *Homo Erectus*, in East Asia have been found in China. The 'Peking Man', a skull fossil discovered in 1927 CE near Beijing, is estimated to have lived in the area 700,000 to 200,000 years ago; the fossilised remains of the 'Yuanmou Man' found in Yuanmou in 1965 CE have been dated to 1.7 million years ago.[10] The presence of ancient lineage hominids and human beings in China, with a high level of sophistication in early culture, which continued through the millennia, is corroborated through scientific findings; this is evident in the discoveries right up to 2001 CE when more than 20 skeletons, along with an altar, pottery, and stone and jade utensils, were found in the Henan province, buried over a wide area indicative of a village, under thick layers of silt deposits from the Yellow river.[11]

From these small villages and farming communities, especially along the Yellow river, grew the concept of a centralised government, the first of which was in the prehistoric Xia Dynasty (c. 2070-1600 BCE). For long, the Xia Dynasty was believed to be more a myth than factual, until excavations in the 1960s and 1970s CE uncovered sites which strongly pointed towards its being of the Bronze Age in China. The spread of civilisation began thereafter (c.1600-221 BCE) along the Yellow river in the Shang era, and spread from there when the Bronze Age culture reached its peak. Traditional Chinese philosophies such as Confucianism and Daoism, developed in the feudal Zhou era, as China expanded into many feudal states and an increase in population. Ancient China finally broke up into warring kingdoms for 200 years, and its reunification marked the beginning of the age of imperial China.[12]

Imperial China

The Imperial China period (c. 221 BCE-1912 CE) makes up the major part of ancient Chinese history. Dynastic rule as centralised feudal empires, began with the Qin Dynasty in 221 BC and continued until the collapse of the Qing Dynasty in 1912. With the recurring rise and fall of dynasties, combined with restructuring after the many uprisings and conquests, Chinese civilisation developed and prospered in times of peace. At the start of this period, the Qin and Han Dynasties established a number of institutions that are considered to be the foundation of the basic political system of a unified country under a single emperor rather than a clan, and the introduction of bureaucracy. It was during the Han Dynasty, the longest imperial dynasty (c. 206 BCE-220 CE) in ancient Chinese history, that the Silk Road trade commenced, connecting China with Central Asia and Europe; agriculture, handicrafts, and commerce developed; and the teachings of Confucius were adopted for governance as the official doctrine. The Han Dynasty was, by far, the most powerful, important, and influential dynasty of ancient China, until its decline.[13]

The fall of the Han Dynasty triggered by natural disasters and rebellions, was the beginning of what is known as China's Dark Ages (c. 220-581CE); the country split into three kingdoms, followed by the rise of the Jin Dynasty (c. 265-420 CE), which, after a weak and shaky hold on the country, once again broke in to the Southern and Northern clans (c. 420-589 CE). These years were chaotic and barbaric during which many religions, primary of which was Buddhism, emerged in northern China. After almost 400 years, another dynasty, the Sui Dynasty (c. 589-618 CE), rose to assume power, although for a short period, but unified the country.[14]

Medieval China

Medieval China moved ahead from internecine warring kingdoms to a unified nation under the Sui Dynasty, seeing steady growth and becoming a culturally and technologically developed nation. The Han Dynasty had been forgotten, and, other, shorter-lived dynasties, such as the Wei, Jin and Wu Hu, assumed control of the government in turn and initiated changes for the good, until the Sui Dynasty took over control and unified the country in 589 CE.[15]

The Sui Dynasty put in place a highly efficient bureaucracy which streamlined governance, leading to an effortless maintenance of the empire. Completion of the Grand Canal, enlargement and rebuilding of portions of the Great Wall are the highlights of the rule of Emperor Wen, and later his son, Yang. Additionally, under their rule, the army was increased to being the largest recorded in the world at that time, and coinage for trade was standardised across the land. Along with the development of infrastructure, the military and the economy, literature too flourished during the Sui Dynasty. The dynasty, however, did not last too long; due to heavy expenditures incurred in the building projects and military expeditions, an uprising, during which Yang was assassinated, marked the culmination of the Sui Dynasty.[16]

The Tang Dynasty (c. 618-907 CE) that followed the Sui Dynasty, is considered to be the golden age of Chinese civilisation. During its rule of three centuries, governance was made more efficient, with a proliferation of poetry, painting, tri-coloured glazed pottery, and wood-block printing. If the Sui Dynasty had started the system of an imperial examination to select the best for the bureaucracy, the Tang Dynasty optimised it, which, with modifications over the centuries, continues to be in use in the Chinese government till the present day. Having done away with the excessive and expensive military operations and the infrastructure projects of the predecessors, the empire had sufficient funds for the upliftment of the general populace. Notwithstanding the efficient rule, the first emperor, Gao-Tzu, was assassinated by his son, Li-Shimin, in 626 CE; to obviate any claimants to the throne, all his brothers and other members of the noble house were also eliminated by him, who then assumed the title of Emperor Taizong (c. 626-649 CE).[17]

Although known for his rationalist outlook and being a scholar of logic and scientific reason, deriding superstitions, Taizong continued, and built upon, the earlier conceptions of ancestor worship and the 'Mandate of Heaven'; Taizong claimed 'divine will' in his actions and announced that those eliminated were now his advisers in their next world![18] He, nevertheless, proved to be a surprisingly efficient ruler, as well as a capable military strategist and warrior; his coup, thus, was not defied as he set about efficiently managing his vast empire.

In following his father's example, Taizong kept much of what was good from the Sui Dynasty, while continuing to improve upon it. This was most visible, especially in Taizong's legal code, which not only emulated Sui concepts, but also provided explicit explanations for connecting crime and punishment. He, however, disregarded his father's concept for foreign policy, and launched a series of successful military campaigns, which not just expanded and secured his empire, but also served to spread his legal code and the Chinese culture. A glowing tribute and a venerated account of his court, the *Zhenguan zhengyao*, written in 708-710 CE, presents a utopian model of an ideal government.[19] It portrays the emperor as powerful and decisive, governing with the aid of a group of talented and well-chosen chief ministers, further depicting him as receptive to their candid opinions, advice and arguments, and as considerate toward the feelings of his people.

On his death in 649 CE, Taizon was succeeded by his son, who christened himself as Emperor Gaozong (649-683 CE), whose wife Wu Zetian was the only empress in the history of China. Her reign during the Tang Dynasty, was not just one of the most effective, but also shrouded in controversies in China's history; she started her own dynasty, the Zhou Dynasty, and called her reign *Tianzhou* (Granted by Heaven). She proclaimed herself as an incarnation of Maitreya Buddha, calling herself Empress Shengsen, translated as 'Holy Spirit'.[20] To ensure the security of her reign, any surviving members of the Tang Dynasty were either made captive or put to death; secret police and spies were placed throughout the country, and in the court to warn her of any attempts of brewing rebellions.

Notwithstanding her reputation of being shrewd and cruel, Empress Wu ensured that no area of Chinese life was left untouched; her reforms were popular because she implemented the suggestions put forth by the people, which reached her directly without going through a bureaucratic labyrinth. Appointment of dedicated teachers with simultaneous reorganisation of the departmental bureaucracy was another improvement towards the education system; similarly, a reformation in the department of agriculture, with a streamlining of the taxation process ensured increased production of crops with a reduction in the taxes for the people. The military too, did not escape her scrutiny and military exams were mandated for the commanders to display their expertise in planning and decision-making. Her campaigns against Korea were a success and inspired confidence in the military generals. Trade, which had been stopped due to the outbreak of plague in 682 CE and raids by the nomads along the route, once again flourished on the Silk Road.[21] Like all dynasties, this too faded away due to various reasons, primarily the old age and paranoia of the empress.

After the Tang Dynasty, there was half a century of division between 907-960 CE, the era being known as the Five Dynasties and Ten Kingdoms period. The period ended with the rise of the Song Dynasty (960-1127 CE), which once again unified central and southern China. The Song era was a period of technological advances and prosperity, with a boom in the domestic and foreign trade, wherein the handicraft industry was the main beneficiary; the four great inventions from China, namely, paper, printing, compass, and gunpowder were also further developed during the Song rule. China, once again, gained stability; institutions, laws, customs were further organised and blended with Chinese culture under the influence of neo-Confucianism—a combination of Buddhism and Taoism—and were popularly accepted.[22] Despite the stability and progress in the country, however, the age-old conflict between the landowners and farmers who tilled the land, continued through the centuries that followed.[23]

Genghis Khan changed China's history by bringing the nation under Mongol rule, after he had unified all the tribes of Mongolia and established the Mongol Khanate, a political entity equivalent to a tribal chiefdom, kingdom, or an empire. The Mongol Empire was divided into four Khanates; the Yuan Dynasty (c. 1279-1368 CE) in China, also known as the Great Khanate, was started by Kublai Khan, the grandson of Genghis Khan.[24] The seat of Yuan rule was in Dadu, modern-day Beijing; this was the capital of the first foreign-led dynasty. As the Mongol Empire expanded, trade, technological advancements, and travel to and from foreign countries continued; Marco Polo from Venice, travelled extensively through China and later described the country in his book, *Travels*[25]. Marco Polo was not the first European to travel to China, but he was the first to explore some remote parts of Asia, leaving detailed chronicles of his travels. His chronicles contain descriptions of what he saw, rather than what he heard about, and contained specifics such as the use of currencies, salt production and collection of revenues. Marco Polo spent more than two decades in the service of Kublai Khan, travelling extensively to the interiors to help in the governance of the country.[26] Kublai Khan died in 1294, and the mantle of leading the Yuan Dynasty was shouldered by his grandson, Temur, who ruled until his death in 1307 (not to be confused with Timur aka Timur Lang, b. 1336, of Uzbekistan, who invaded India). The dynasty continued until 1368 when the Red Turban rebellions (the Red Turban Army traditionally wore red turbans and carried red banners) against the Yuan Dynasty, between 1351 and 1368, eventually ended the Mongol rule in China.[27]

After a series of natural disasters and the Red Turban rebellions, led by the Han people, a new ethnic Chinese Dynasty emerged, the Ming dynasty (1368-1644 CE). The Ming dynastic rule was a period of Chinese strength and prosperity during which international trade was promoted and several voyages to the West were undertaken. The Ming dynasty is also remembered for its drama, literature, and world-renowned porcelain. Emperor Taizu, the founder of the dynasty rose from a humble background, rising through a rebellion to defeat the Mongolian rulers and start the Ming dynasty. A man with a fierce sense of justice and military discipline, he was also very suspicious of his officials; an investigation that began in 1380 CE, lasted for 14 years and led to about 30,000 executions![28] Taizu was succeeded by his son, Chengzu, who expanded the tribute system to other nations, which was then replaced by maritime trade in 1557. A much-in-demand product in the European countries, was the fine-quality porcelain produced during the Ming years; although the production had started during the Tang Dynasty, the production process was refined in the Ming era.[29] Like all previous dynasties, the Ming dynasty, too, faltered and finally succumbed to greedy leadership and fiscal problems arising as the after-effects of natural disasters; this led to peasant uprisings and the repeated Manchu invasions from the northeast, which finally culminated in the downfall of the Ming dynasty.[30]

Approaching Modern Times

During the waning years of the Ming dynasty, the Manchus, from Manchuria, north of the Great Wall, continually attacked China for three generations, until they finally established the Qing Dynasty (c. 1644-1912 CE), which also proved to be the last imperial dynasty of China, being overthrown by the Republic of China; this is also known as the Manchu Dynasty. Though, initially harsh in their treatment of the people, executing everyone suspected of disloyalty, the Manchus later restored certain practices of their predecessors; the civil services examinations were recommenced, but only the Manchus were permitted to hold high offices. China experienced growth and peace for about 150 years under the Qing Dynasty.

Notwithstanding the peace in the country, China remained aloof, to some extent, from the outside world; trade was restricted to a few items, foreign ambassadors were not permitted entry to the capital, and in order to keep European influence out of the country, the Qing emperors also made Christianity unlawful in the 1800s. Culture flourished and religion, with Buddhism at the helm, was widespread; the period under the rule of Emperor Kangxi (1661-1722 CE) and Emperor Qianlong (1735-1796 CE) is considered as the 'golden age of prosperity' in Chinese history.[31] However, within the society, discrimination between the largest sect, the Hans, and the ruling sect, the Manchus, became widespread; a Han was not permitted to marry a Manchu! Such bias created discontent amongst the people and eventually led to the weakening of the dynasty and its downfall.

The Opium Wars

Opium was introduced in China by the Turkish and Arab traders in the late 6th century CE. It was used medicinally, to relieve pain and to de-stress, albeit in limited quantities, until the 17th century. In the early 18th century, the Portuguese realised that they could make profits by importing opium from India and then selling it in China; the British discovered this method in 1773 CE and became the leading supplier in the Chinese market.

Other Western nations too joined in, including USA, which procured it from Turkey as well. Addiction to opium had already increased in China, when smoking tobacco was introduced from North America, and opium was added to it. With the proliferation in the supply of the drug from various sources, addiction increased, leading to a big jump in the import of the drug. Seeing the scale and ubiquity of opium addiction amongst the people and even the imperial army, a total prohibition on the import and use of opium within the country was imposed by Emperor Jiaqing, in 1796. Despite such rulings, the opium trade continued to thrive through rampant smuggling.[32]

There was an ulterior motive for Britain and other European countries to undertake the opium trade; the countries suffered from a continual trade imbalance with China. The Western nations had a huge demand for Chinese tea, silk, and porcelain pottery, but there was correspondingly hardly any demand for Europe's manufactured goods and other trade items in China, as a result of which, payment for Chinese products was made in either gold or silver. The opium trade, which created an unending demand among Chinese addicts, resolved this chronic trade imbalance; the quantity brought into China increased from about 200 chests annually in 1729 CE to roughly 1,000 chests in 1767 CE, further increasing to about 10,000 per year between 1820 CE and 1830 CE![33]

Licenced traders of the East India Company had streamlined the supply source from Bengal, in India, and the distribution was managed through the active cooperation of corrupt officials of the Chinese government. The stringent efforts of the Qing Dynasty to enforce its decrees on the sale of opium did not succeed, and resulted in two wars with Britain, both of which ended in defeat for China. The first war, between Britain and China (1839-1842 CE) ended with the fall of Nanking and the subsequent signing of the Treaty of Nanking. While China did not legalise the trade, it did have to halt its efforts to stop it; China was also forced to pay reparations for the war and the destruction of opium, and cede the island of Hong Kong to Britain in perpetuity. The second Opium War (1856-1860 CE), fought between an Anglo-French alliance and China, resulted in the signing of two treaties, namely, the Treaty of Tientsin in 1858, and the Convention of Peking in 1860; under the former, foreigners were granted greater freedom of movement within China and the latter ratified the former treaty and ceded the Kowloon peninsula, also in permanence; the Chinese government was also compelled to decriminalise the opium trade, but was permitted to impose a small import tax on the narcotic.[34]

Decline of the Qing Dynasty

The decline of the Qing Dynasty was triggered by the two Opium Wars; rebellions, though suppressed, occurred in many parts of the country until almost the end of the century, devastating floods in the Yellow river in 1887 CE, and the rise of Japan under Emperor Meiji in 1868 CE, which then led to the first Sino-Japanese War (1894-1895 CE), also contributed in no small measure to the consequent famine and a poor economy. China lost the war against Japan too, leading to another round of humiliating concessions, as had happened after the Opium Wars; it was forced to recognise Korea (Joseon Dynasty) as an independent nation, grant trade concessions to Japan as it had done with the Western nations after the Opium Wars, and part with the Liadong peninsula, the Penghu archipelago, and Taiwan (then known as Formosa), by the Treaty of Shimonoseki of April 1895 CE.[35]

The Boxer Rebellion was an anti-imperialism, anti-foreign, and anti-Christian revolt; it was an indigenous peasant uprising to rid the country of foreign influence between 1899 CE and 1901 CE, wherein foreign missionaries and Chinese Christians were murdered. The name 'Boxer' was of a Militia United of Righteousness (*Yihequan*); its members had knowledge of Chinese martial arts, which were referred to as 'Chinese Boxing' by the Western nations of that era.[36] When the Boxers entered Peking (now Beijing) and barricaded the diplomatic enclave in which foreigners and missionaries had taken refuge, an expeditionary force of an eight-nation alliance—Japan, Russia, Britain, Italy, Germany, France, America, and Austria—went in to relieve the siege, but were beaten back by the rebel and Qing troops. A strengthened alliance force, now of 11 nations, fought a fierce battle against the Chinese Army, which by then included the Boxers in its ranks. The Chinese Army was defeated, Peking and Tianjin were occupied by the foreign forces, the siege in Peking was lifted and another treaty, the Boxer Protocol, was signed, inflicting heavy penalties on China.[37]

In the aftermath of the Boxer Rebellion, the Qing court put in place some all-encompassing reforms, one of which included the termination of the many centuries old examination system; as it always happens when radical changes are proposed, some felt the proposed changes were far too many, while there were others who felt the opposite. Young officials, including military officers, and students, were, however, debating on a different reform altogether, that of establishing a constitutional monarchy, or an end to the dynastic rule in the country with the creation of a republic; public opinion, influenced by some intellectuals and the revolutionary ideas of Sun Yat-sen, was the main source of their inspiration. A localised military uprising in Wuchang (a part of Wuhan today) lit the fire of the revolution, which soon spread and the Republic of China was proclaimed on January 1, 1912, ending 2,000 years of dynastic rule.[38]

The End of Dynastic Rule

With the end of dynastic rule, the history of the Republic of China, as a constitutional republic commences (1912-1949 CE). As is with any nation that changes over to a new political system, it was with China too; the country faced many trials and tribulations in the initial years at the hands of both external and internal forces—foreign nations and warlord generals—who still aspired to control China!

Among the many revolutionary groups, influenced by intellectuals and political reformers, one that was led by an anti-Qing activist, Sun Yat-sen, was progressively becoming popular amongst overseas Chinese, which included students. Flush with funds provided by the diaspora, Sun Yat-sen had formed a reformist group in Tokyo, as early as 1905 CE, and included Huang Xing, another popular leader; this group also had some regional military officers and other reformers who had fled persecution in China, when the Qing Dynasty had initiated its own reforms. Sun Yat-sen announced his political principles in 1905 CE, although he had conceptualised them much earlier in 1897; his philosophy was centred on making China a free, prosperous and a powerful nation, free from any foreign interference. These principles, often recapitulated as nationalism, democracy, and the livelihood of the people, became the foundation of the policy of the Republic of China, and are also included in the Chinese national anthem.[39]

Notwithstanding the election of Sun Yat-sen as the first provisional president of China and the general acceptance of his philosophy, he was not able to garner enough support from the other provinces and from within the military, which was under the strong leadership of General Yuan Shih-kai. To prevent the country drifting into a civil war, Sun Yat-sen abdicated his position and handed over the president's post to Yuan Shih-kai, a man with an unbridled ambition to rule the nation himself, which eventually led to his downfall.

Yuan Shih-kai may have been a strong leader in the army, but he was corrupt and abused power, to the extent that he eventually dismantled the Parliament to make himself the supreme ruler and declared himself the emperor. All individuals opposed to him were put to death, but several provinces did oppose him and declared independence from him. The opposing provinces united and formed the National Protection Army that revolted against his rule. Several generals of Yuan Shih-kai, who were provincial governors and unhappy with him declaring himself as emperor, did not resist the uprising. This rebellion, and other reasons of misrule, such as disregard of republican institutions put in place by his predecessors, dissolution of the ruling Kuomintang (KMT) Party, and ignoring the provisional Constitution, led to the fall of Yuan Shih-kai's rule; he abdicated on March 22, 1916.[40]

After the brief rule of Yuan Shih-kai, a power vacuum was created; several provinces declared their independence and China declined into warlord states from 1916 to 1928. The warlord period in Chinese history is a period of chaos, corruption, political and military alignments, suspicions and betrayals, which ended with Sun Yat-sen re-emerging from his exile in Japan and advocating reunification. Sun Yat-sen returned from Japan in 1917 CE and in 1921 CE, started a self-proclaimed military government in Guangzhou.[41] Convinced that the only path to reunify China was through a military campaign from his base in the south, followed by political tutelage, he first resurrected his earlier disbanded party, the KMT—later renamed as the Nationalist Party of China—and then initiated cooperation with the Communist Party of China (CPC—but commonly known as the CCP) with the admission of Communist members into his party, but only as individuals; the CCP was not included as an organised bloc.[42]

Sun Yat-sen established his rule with all the associated issues such as finance concerns, building military power, and planting the seed of nationalism in the Chinese people. In January 1923, he signed a manifesto with the Soviets, which asserted that while the Soviet system was not suitable for China, the Soviet Union would, however, assist the KMT in the efforts to unify China; following the signing of the manifesto, Chiang Kai-shek was sent to the Soviet Union to study the military and political systems there, thus, establishing a strong foundation for cooperation. In a crucial decision, Sun Yat-sen also decided to align the KMT and the Soviets, with the CCP, which had been formed in 1921.[43]

Sun Yat-sen was unfortunate not to see the fruits of his labour; he died of an illness in March 1925, but not before reiterating his 'Three Principles', which later became a part of the national anthem of the Republic of China. As often happens in a movement based on a single personality, happened in the case of the KMT too. A power struggle ensued between Sun Yat-sen's protégé, Chiang Kai-shek, and one of his old revolutionary comrades, Wang Jingwei, which saw a split in the KMT.

With the KMT being able to firmly exercise its authority and the growth of its military, the struggle to control the party's ideology and, hence, its direction, grew. On one side were the right-wing nationalists under Chiang Kai-shek, and on the other side were Wang Jingwei with his left-wing allies, along with the CCP and Soviet assistance. An anti-Communist government was established in Nanjing and the CCP was able to stabilise its forces in Wuhan. Alarmed at the growth of the Communists, Chiang began a systematic elimination of their influence beginning May 1926 in Guangzhou and continuing to April 1927, when a violent, full-scale purge of Communists took place in Shanghai, known as the 'Shanghai Massacre' in Chinese history books. These events led to a total split between the right-wing faction under Chiang Kai-shek, and the left-wing faction under Wang Jingwei within the KMT. These incidents also led to an end of the alliance between the KMT and CCP, and can be said to be the beginning of the Chinese civil war between the two factions. In mid-1927, the CCP was driven out of Wuhan and the KMT under Chiang Kai-shek gained full control over the whole of China. Chiang Kai-shek, singly, exercised total control as the most powerful man in China, with his government being recognised internationally. Improvement in the country was initiated through several reforms and policies, leading to record growth in the economy, and the development of democracy.[44]

The decade ending in 1937 is considered to be the 'golden decade' in modern Chinese history, with the KMT in full control of the country and being able to implement its programme of building a modern China. Although it did face a variety of political, diplomatic, economic, and military problems, these were overcome and gradually the rule, in conformity with the principles of its founder, Sun Yat-sen, settled down. Nevertheless, during this period of growth and development, some serious insurgencies/wars did occur, some of which were as follows: the Kumul Rebellion, between 1931-1934, which was an uprising by the Uighurs, loyal to the Kumul Khanate, who wanted to re-establish the Khanate in Xinjiang; the Sino-Tibetan War which began in 1930 under the 13th Dalai Lama in a dispute over the boundary between Tibet and China, with Tibet claiming the adjoining lands of China that were inhabited by its people; and the Soviet invasion of Xinjiang in 1934, when the Chinese Army was on the verge of overrunning the Soviet assisted troops in the Kumul Rebellion.[45]

Few Chinese had any doubts about Japan eyeing the vast resources of China. Desperate for raw materials for its industry and pressure by a growing population, Japan annexed Manchuria in 1931 and established a puppet government led by an ex-Qing emperor. This was a big blow to the KMT government, which complained to the international community; Japan, however, was defiant. The people of China were upset at the Japanese advance, but more with their own government, which was preoccupied with the extermination of the Communists. Chiang Kai-shek was detained by his own generals and forced into an alliance with the Communists to fight a common enemy, the invading Japanese Army.[46]

The unity between the KMT and the Communists had beneficial effects on the under-pressure CCP. Notwithstanding Japan's steady advance in northern China, and the coastal regions, the conflicts between the KMT and CCP became more frequent in areas not under Japan's control. With USA entering the Pacific theatre during World War II, in 1941, the nature of their relationship changed. The CCP expanded its influence wherever and whenever it sensed openings, through mass gatherings, administrative and land-and-tax reforms, and the spread of its organisational network, while the KMT concentrated on its rather unsuccessful attempts to neutralise the spread of Communist influence.

During and after World War II, China emerged as a symbolic military power, with USA playing a major role in Chinese affairs, primarily to contain the spread of Communism. China's emergence as a great power was far from reality; in actuality, the nation was economically drained out by the military demands of a foreign war and internal conflicts, leading to rising inflation, hoarding and profiteering by unscrupulous members of the Nationalist Party (KMT); a famine in the wake of the war, and floods led to dissatisfaction in many parts of the country. The situation was further complicated on the geopolitical front, when after the Yalta Conference in February 1945, Soviet troops entered Manchuria to bring an early end to the war against Japan; while China was not present at Yalta, it had been consulted and had given its consent, believing that the Soviet Union would interact only with the KMT government.[47]

When World War II ended in August 1945, it was an indication of peace to prevail, both for USA and Japan; however, for China, it signalled the start of a conflict between Chiang Kai-shek's KMT and Mao Zedong's (then known as Mao Tse-tung, and generally known as Mao) CCP, with each trying to gain the advantage in north and northeast China (Manchuria). This civil war was fought in the backdrop of an international tussle between USA and Soviet Union, wherein the two nations were trying to further their own interests in China—USA siding with the KMT and the Soviet Union with the CCP. It is interesting to note that both the KMT and CCP, while battling each other, using whatever limited military backing that was offered to them by their benefactors, were also talking with each other, pushed into negotiations by the two foreign nations—a case of 'talking while fighting'![48]

The negotiations between two ideologically strong opponents broke down, the first indications coming by mid-1946; despite a renewed effort to bring the two parties back to the table, a full-blown war broke out between the KMT and CCP in January 1947. The fighting spread from the south to northeast China, in both rural and urban areas. For the KMT, the situation deteriorated rapidly, for the CCP was no longer a mere guerrilla force; by the end of 1948, through the winter to 1949, the CCP won three major battles against Chiang Kai-shek's army: the Liao-Shen, Ping-Jin, and Huai-Hai campaigns, forcing the government to move from Nanjing, to Chongqing, then to Chengdu, then Xichang, and finally to Taiwan. On October 1, 1949, the Communist Party, led by Mao, formed the People's Republic of China (PRC), while Chiang Kai-shek, with his troops and sympathiser-refugees, established the Republic of China (ROC), with Taipei as the seat of the government.

History of the People's Republic of China

The two Chinas have continued to exist since 1949, each claiming to be the true representative of the people. The PRC on the mainland, continued to grow into a major power, and has been, for seven decades, synonymous with China. The ROC, being the enemy of Communist China on the mainland, was the recipient of massive American aid, both economic and military from the 1950s and has been, since then, a protégé of USA. Due to the controversial nature of the political status of the ROC that has continued to exist from the day of its inception, it is recognised by only 14 of the 193 UN member nations as the legitimate government of China, much to the chagrin of the PRC; nevertheless, it has grown to be a major economic power in Asia.

The history of the PRC is the history of mainland China, starting from 1949, under the CCP. Just as it was during the dynastic rule, when the power flowed from one dynasty to another, it is now known as the periods of rule under the 'paramount leaders', as the elected leaders of the CCP are known. The paramount leaders of the PRC have been Mao Zedong (1949-1976), Hua Guofeng (1976-1978) was an interim leader during a transition, Deng Xiaoping (1978-1989), Jiang Xemin (1989-2002), Hu Jintao (2002-2012), and Xi Jinping (2012 to the present), each leaving his mark while governing China, in his own unique style.

The time period in Chinese history, between 1949, when the CCP under Mao gained victory over the nationalist KMT, to 1976, the year of Mao's death, is commonly known as Maoist China. Mao had inherited a China that had been ravaged by foreign invasions, civil wars and natural disasters, for almost a century. Both urban and rural communities, along with agriculture and industry, had, therefore, to be rebuilt from scratch, although the methodology was controversial. Mao's government carried out land reforms, a movement that had begun during the last stages of the civil war, and involved mass murders of landowners by the tenants, and thereafter redistribution of the land to form communes—a system of collective ownership—rather than individual ownership. The Soviet model of five-year plans was followed for the revival of industry, and industries were nationalised and transferred from private to public enterprises.

Coming on the heels of the civil war, China was involved in the war in Korea in the summer of 1950. Both the Soviet Union and China did not wish to see a UN-backed Korea on its border, taking it to be a political and military victory for USA. With the Soviet Union displaying its reluctance to enter the war against USA, it was left to China to stall the advance of the UN forces. Though poorly equipped, China had the luxury of huge reserves of manpower, and sent in waves of troops to the South, some of whom were veterans of the civil war, but a majority were inexperienced in modern warfare and lacked modern weaponry. Notwithstanding the massive casualties that the Chinese troops suffered, China showed to USA that while it may be a new and emerging nation, it was a force to reckon with.

As a fallout of the Korean War, the possibility of normalising relations with USA were bleak; hence, to get back to the task of building a new nation, China leaned towards the Soviet Union, accepting considerable economic and military aid, though with not the smoothest of relations with its leadership, even here!

As socialism was gradually accepted by the general public by 1956, Mao decided to take a tolerant view of the governance by giving the coming years for consolidation, although worried about bureaucratic hurdles. In February 1957, just after the 8th Congress of the CCP, Mao, in one of his most famous speeches, announced, "Let a hundred flowers bloom, let a hundred schools of thought contend".[49] The CCP took it upon itself to encourage the 'Hundred Flowers Campaign', to further spread the socialist way of life, but there were many who disagreed and openly voiced their dissent against the Party's rule. Taken aback at the widespread criticism, Mao ended the campaign and commenced a purge of all suspected dissenters, who he termed as 'Rightists within the Party'; Xi Jinping, the present Party leader since 2012, was also a victim of Mao's excesses, when his father, once a leading revolutionary, was branded as a conspirator and jailed for his bourgeois background and Xi, then a 15-year-old, was despatched to a distant village to work in an agricultural commune![50] It is estimated that about half a million people were persecuted—eliminated, jailed, or simply disappeared—during 1957-1958, of whom many were intellectuals or leaders in the government![51]

The Great Leap Forward

The Great Leap Forward was a social, cultural, and economic crusade initiated by Mao in 1958, towards the end of the 'great purge', wherein Mao wanted to transform China from a predominantly agrarian society to a Communist society with the creation of people's communes; it was his vision to increase the agricultural output and also bring industry to the rural areas. Scared of being branded as rightists, officials at both local and higher positions, did not dare report shortfalls in production while collecting all the grain from the farmers, at times leaving them to starve; rural industrialisation, although a priority, was also a non-starter, as Mao insisted on producing steel in backyard furnaces, which at best, could churn out only lumps of pig-iron. While the focus of the Great Leap was to enhance development of China's agricultural and industrial sectors parallelly, lopsided policies led to a disaster in both sectors, resulting in many deaths, estimates ranging from 15 to 50 million![52]

Mao, however, did not withdraw from his policies, instead blaming 'rightists' for the failure, through poor implementation of his instructions. In a renewed effort to purge the suspected bourgeois, who he perceived had infiltrated the rank and file of his socialist movement, he launched a fresh drive in 1963 to educate the masses, and started a Cultural Revolution in 1966 that lasted until his death in 1976; the primary goal was to preserve the true Communist ideology, and steer the people towards Mao's thoughts, through the mobilisation of the youth, called the Red Guards, who had been told that "to rebel is justified".[53] The Cultural Revolution involved violent struggles between factions, which were often quelled by the People's Liberation Army (PLA). Mao suggested the end of the revolution in 1969 once he realised that the country was in chaos and spinning out of control, but the active phase continued till much later, under the leadership of Mao's wife, Jiang Qing. She, and her three co-conspirators (known as the

Gang of Four), who had aspirations of continuing to lead China after Mao, controlled most of China's media and criticised the moderates such as Deng Xiaoping and Zhou Enlai, to the extent of even despatching the former to a re-education camp.[54]

The death of Zhou Enlai in January 1976, can be said to be the beginning of the end of the Cultural Revolution. Widespread grief over Zhou Enlai's death, resentment against the propaganda generated by Jiang Qing against Zhou Enlai, and restrictions against public mourning, turned into huge demonstrations, with public denouncements of Mao and his wife and even the Cultural Revolution; the memorial service on April 4, held at the Tiananmen Square in Beijing on the traditional day of mourning, witnessed a gathering of thousands, rattling the confidence of Jiang Qing and her accomplices. Widespread riots reported from Beijing and many other cities, were attributed to Deng Xiaoping, who, for the second time in 10 years was purged and removed from all official posts by Jiang Qing. On the death of Mao in September 1976, his hand-picked successor, Hua Guofeng, had the Gang of Four arrested, indicating the end of the Cultural Revolution; officially though, it was declared over in the 11th Party Congress in August 1977.[55]

Post-Mao Era

Uncertainty prevailed over Mao's policies and the vestiges of the Cultural Revolution. This was reflected in the choice of the members of the Political Bureau preferred just after the 11th Party Congress had convened in August 1977. Like Hua Guofeng, a relatively unknown entity until his appointment by Mao as premier on the death of Zhou Enlai, most of the members were individuals whose careers had benefited from the Cultural Revolution; the other half were those persecuted, like Deng Xiaoping, but now 'rehabilitated'; deft political manoeuvring quickly turned the tide in favour of the latter group, with Deng Xiaoping emerging as the vice-premier and the second-most powerful figure in the Party only to become the paramount leader of China in 1978.[56]

Deng Xiaoping took over leadership of China during the chaotic aftermath of the Cultural Revolution. While the reforms had been initiated by Hua Guofeng, after Mao's death in 1976, it was Deng's steadying influence as the vice-premier, that gave the reforms a clear direction; with his economic prudence to pace the reforms, he maintained the support of those who feared the opening of markets, as well as those who feared that the opening would be too slow. Deng Xiaoping enjoyed the popular support of the Party senior cadre notwithstanding the persecution he suffered at the hands of Mao and the Gang of Four. Deng and his protégés operated through a process of consensus, compromise and persuasion, to engineer a radical change that Deng would later call China's "Second Revolution".[57]

By the early 1980s, the Chinese leadership, having established itself, began to loosen the stranglehold that the State had over China's economic and political systems since the 1950s. In the economic domain, the easing of the rules translated into a transition from a commandeered economy to a more market-driven economy; powers were decentralised to provincial and local officials with a removal of political oversight on their economic activities, thus, reducing interference from the central authorities in Beijing. Markets were gradually opened to Foreign Direct Investment (FDI) and by 1984, 14 port cities were declared as Special Economic Zones (SEZs) to encourage foreign investment. Deng restored domestic political stability, even if it asked for the use of force to quell protests, believing that a country could move ahead on the path of democracy depending upon how stable the political situation was. Under his leadership, China developed into a rapidly growing economy, with accompanied rising standards of living, thus, elevating millions out of poverty, considerably boosting personal and cultural freedoms, and with growing ties to the world economy. Deng also left in place a mildly authoritarian government that remained committed to the CCP's one-Party rule even while it relied on free-market mechanisms to transform China into a developed country.[58]

After the infamous violent suppression by the army of the student's demonstration in Tiananmen Square in Beijing, and also in other cities, in mid-1989, there was a reshuffle in the top leadership; Jiang Zemin, a comparatively more authoritarian leader, became the general secretary, followed by his taking over as chairman of the Military Commission. In 1993, he was elected as the president of China, by the National People's Congress, and then declared as the paramount leader on the death of Deng Xiaoping in 1997. Working ahead on the political reforms that were underway, he, for the first time, invited successful business people to join the CCP. Under Jiang's stewardship, China joined the World Trade Organisation (WTO) in 2001, and encouraged the country's state-owned enterprises to venture out into the world to satiate China's growing appetite for raw materials, so needed for its growing economy. After serving the maximum two five-year terms, Jiang Zemin stepped down from the posts of general secretary of the Party in 2002, and president in 2003, handing over the reins to Hu Jintao; Jiang Zemin finally stepped down from the chairmanship of the Military Commission in 2004, in favour of Hu Jintao.[59]

Hu Jintao became the president of China in 2003, after probably the smoothest transition process. Hu's tenure was marked with challenges and efforts to further reform the political and economic systems. The first major challenge his government had to face was the outbreak of the SARS epidemic, which had begun to spread right after he assumed office in March 2003. After some initial hesitation in making announcements, he acted decisively and imposed restrictions to control the spread; the actions taken by Hu Jintao included the dismissal of the health minister for hiding the outbreak, which in itself was a first! Tentatively and with caution, he took steps to open up the government, inviting debates on topics from the public, before putting them to vote; journalists were permitted to attend some meetings and more news conferences were held than in the previous years. Work to reduce poverty, build a harmonious society with an equitable distribution of wealth, transparency and discipline in the Party cadre, were some of his key areas of thrust; however, many of his actions appeared to be in consonance with the precept that stability and removal of threats to the Party were his prime responsibilities. In the mid-2000s, however, Hu devolved more authority to the security and police forces to crack down even on alleged threats to the Party's hold on power, following which dissidents and activists along with Chinese and foreign journalists were detained, and use of the internet, free speech, and civil liberties were curbed. At celebrations in Beijing to mark 30 years of the beginning of the "reform and opening" policy initiated by Deng Xiaoping in 1978, Hu promised that China would open up more but, the language was filled with Marxist-Leninist jargon, which asserted that the Communist Party would remain in control. "Without stability, we can do nothing and [we will] lose what has been achieved," he said. "Our Party will...remain the backbone of all the nation's ethnic groups in dealing with various foreign and domestic risks and tests."[60]

David E. Sanger and Michael Wines wrote in the *New York Times*, "China has become a $5 trillion industrial colossus, a growing military force, and, it sometimes appears, a model of authoritarian decisiveness, navigating out of the global financial crisis and sealing its position as the world's fastest rising power...China is far wealthier and more influential, but Mr. Hu also may be the weakest leader of the Communist era. He is less able to project authority than his predecessors were. By any measure, Mr. Hu is the most constrained Chinese leader in modern times. The notion that he could engineer a sweeping policy change the way that Mr. Deng threw open China's economy three decades ago is unthinkable; more often, he is a negotiator, brokering deals in a collective leadership where he has never seemed to fully consolidate power".[61]

Contrary to hopes expressed by both Chinese and foreign observers, when Hu Jintao assumed power, the reforms that were talked about and expected, were not actually seen being put into practice; for all its changes, constrained into a quasi-command economy, the administration ignored legal protections and expanded the state security apparatus. Ian Johnson and Keith Bradsher wrote in the *New York Times*: "Many economists have begun to question, however, whether Mr. Hu's tenure has amounted to a 'lost decade' for refashioning China's investment-driven economy into a broader, more stable system. State-owned enterprises have gradually strengthened their roles in the economy through a combination of monopoly power and access to cheap loans from state-owned banks."[62] Hu's government shied away from tolerance, suffocated liberal societal opinion, and strengthened the CCP rather than adjusting its relationship with the people. The era of Hu Jintao (2002-2012) was also seen as one of a "win-win philosophy", where China applied itself ceaselessly to soothe the nerves of its neighbours, and the rest of the world and convince them that its rise would be peaceful and, as its own stature grew, so would that of its partners. The summer of 2008 saw China host the Olympic Games in Beijing, which earned it accolades from the world over; on the domestic front within the political circles, the Olympic Games also consolidated the position of an individual, Xi Jinping, who had overseen the preparations for the mega-event.

Xi Jinping Takes Over Leadership

Hu Jintao stepped down as general secretary of the Party in November 2012, and the Party Congress elected Xi Jinping to the office during the CCP's 18th Congress. Simultaneously, he also handed over charge as chairman of the Military Commission to Xi, who until then had occupied the position of vice chairman of the commission; Xi was elected as president to replace Hu, by the National People's Congress in March 2013. In contrast to his reform-oriented father, who was purged during the Cultural Revolution, Xi Jinping had the reputation for political sagacity and for following the Party line.

Xi Jinping had aired his views on leading the country as far back as in 2000; during an interview, he shared his views, stating that "a new leader needed to continue working on the foundations laid by his predecessor, but, at the same time, come in with his own plans and set an agenda during the first year".[63] Xi set out to rule China with a distinctive style and agenda of his own, and at an accelerated pace. Starting as the general secretary and then as the president, Xi Jinping's tenure has prominently comprised assuming control of all leading committees and commissions that oversee government policy issues; he, therefore, is today the core leader and is now considered as the most powerful since Mao.

During his climb to the ultimate position of power through the Party ranks, Xi had observed that corruption was central throughout the Party and the economy, hence, as a first step, he initiated a nationwide anti-corruption campaign that soon saw the removal of many high and low officials; demanding personal loyalty from Party and military leaders, he has eliminated rivals through an all-sweeping anti-corruption campaign; his aggressive reforms programme has increased, rather than diminished, the role of the CCP and State in the society and in the economy. China's role in world affairs too, has been a display of assertiveness hithertofore not seen, wherein China has claimed territorial sovereignty over the entire South China Sea (SCS) despite a ruling to the contrary by the Permanent Court of Arbitration in The Hague. In pursuing his economic diplomacy goals, Xi Jinping has promoted the 'One Belt One Road' scheme (also known as the 'Belt and Road Initiative—BRI) for promoting trade through the ancient Silk Route, and developing a sea route too for the same; in the bargain, China has more than a toe-hold in many nations due to their difficulties in repaying the loans, much to the exasperation and misgivings of other developed nations.

Why China Does What it Does: The Influence of History

Many analysts and strategists have often wondered whether the events in Chinese history influence its actions and behaviour today! Some view China as a nation that has not changed over the centuries, thus, misreading historical events, while some view it as possessing the same political and security perceptions over the centuries and dynasties, as it developed through them, reaching what it is today. What is missed in such an analysis, however, is that each succeeding dynasty wrote its predecessor's history, and the central political thought—what is now generically called Confucianism—was based on the concept that ideals for ruling were to be found in the past, with the virtuous ruler matching, or even outdoing them. Performance mattered, but mainly as proof of history's judgment. The reality, however, is much more intricate and needs a detailed view.

As aforementioned, China changed its security and, hence, political perceptions from dynasty to dynasty, varying between periods of strengths and weaknesses; during some such periods the variation was so stark and extensive that even some Chinese historians shy away from making any simplified comparisons of events in history to today's, or even a future governmental policy, much less draw any lessons from those events. Nevertheless, history cannot be totally ignored.

Does history, then, really have an impact on Chinese thinking and behaviour today? Will this influence continue as China's power and sway grow in the future? The lessons of history are echoed in three mind-sets: (1) national pride alongside a strong fear of chaos; (2) an indoctrinated image of a peace-loving and defensive society alongside a strong and virtuous central government; and (3) a unique, hierarchical, yet mutually beneficial, view of inter-state relations.[64] These three perspectives are being discussed in the following paragraphs.

China is a nation that has suffered political, economic, and social chaos linked with the devastations inflicted upon it by the Western powers and Japan, in the 19th and early 20th centuries, a period that is called the 'century of humiliation'; none of the leaders, from Sun Yat-sen to the present-day ones, have forgotten this period, and they have ensured that the people too do not forget it, so as to avenge the humiliation. The emergence of nationalism, through the years, amongst the Chinese who are very proud of their long and ancient history, has prompted them to build their country into a strong, prosperous, and modern society to be included in the front ranks of the major powers. As a result of these concerns, and the yearning for China to again become a powerful and wealthy nation, most Chinese, and their leaders, appreciate a resilient, united, and proudly nationalistic central government led by worthy entities, who keep the people's interests in mind, and would work to avoid the chaos that can be generated through widespread corruption in a weak civil society. The leaders believe, and, in turn, the people are led to believe, that the Western nations may offer developmental tools for progress and prosperity, but these are not suited for China's social and political development.

The second attribute is fed by years of propaganda and an ill-considered and impulsive understanding of the country's history by the leadership, whether Communist or nationalist, and passed on to the public. The country is portrayed as a peace-loving nation, posing no threat to any nation, and rather focussed on protecting its territorial integrity, while working towards internal development. This perception is generated by a long record of unsettled borders and susceptibility to peripheral attacks, combined with the experience of the century of humiliation. Many Chinese today, therefore, view Western dominance (mainly the US) of the world with suspicion, thinking that any action by the West, under the pretext of offering assistance to China, is actually for personal gains and would be detrimental to China's stability and growth.

While the West is generally viewed with suspicion, there are contradictions within a few Chinese minds; the achievements of the Western nations are applauded, albeit secretly, by some from the older, educated generation of intellectuals and political activists. If the current behaviour of USA and its Western allies is considered arrogant and hegemonistic, the pre-1949 relationship with USA is quoted positively.[65] In the hierarchical international order, many in China consider it the responsibility of the larger and developed powers, to guide and mentor the smaller nations in mutually beneficial directions, also as a justification of China's behaviour towards its own smaller, contiguous neighbours. Mutual respect, reverence and admiration, and responsibility, are considered to be a substantial part of the desired inter-state behaviour, and are supposed to reflect not only China's importance in Asia, but also in the general global order.

Many in the Chinese leadership, especially in the current generation led by Xi Jinping, manipulate these concepts to serve their own interests and selfish ends, suppressing history when needed, or even recreating it to serve them in the present. The CCP very nearly pressed the self-destruction button during Mao's Cultural Revolution, but soon recovered after the 1989 massacre in Tiananmen Square, when it promoted itself as the saviour of Chinese culture and traditions; since 2012, after taking over as the general secretary of the Party, Xi Jinping has taken it upon himself to promote traditions, building upon the work of his predecessors, especially Hu Jintao and his call for a Taoist sounding "harmonious society".[66] The leadership strongly believes in the rejuvenation of the country, while reflecting on the five thousand years of history, quoting China's contribution to the development of the world, but being fully aware that, in a socialist—single-party—country, change often occurs when the past is tested. The people are led to believe that China's recognition in the global order as a major, but not necessarily a singular power, is to be respected for peace and harmony. This, of course, is very different from the display of Chinese resurgence, where it is adamant on its domination of the smaller nations in Asia and beyond!

History by definition, is a narrative of the past; it is, however, also China's present and future!

Notes

1. Ian Johnson, "China's Memory Manipulators", *The Guardian*, June 8, 2016, https://www.theguardian.com/world/2016/jun/08/chinas-memory-manipulators, accessed on April 14, 2020.
2. "Ancient China—Dynasties", https://www.ducksters.com/history/china/dynasties.php, accessed on January 10, 2021.

3. "Ancient Civilisation: China", Resource Library Collection, https://www.nationalgeographic.org/topics/resource-library-ancient-civilization-china/?q=&page=1&per_page=25, accessed on January 10, 2021.

4. Joshua J. Mark, "Ancient China," Ancient History Encyclopaedia, Last modified December 18, 2012. https://www.ancient.eu/china/, accessed on April 15, 2020.

5. Ibid.

6. "Cathay", Encyclopaedia Britannica Online, Encyclopaedia Britannica 2009, as quoted in Cathay-Wikipedia, en.m.wikipedia.org, accessed on April 19, 2020.

7. n. 3.

8. Mark, n. 4.

9. Charles E. Greer, "Yellow River", Encyclopaedia Britannica, www.britannica.com, accessed on April 15, 2020.

10. n. 3.

11. Ibid.

12. Ibid.

13. "The History of China: Dynasty/Era Summary, Timeline", China Highlights, https://www.chinahighlights.com/travelguide/culture/china-history.htm#:~:text=The%20ancient%20China%20era%20was%20c.%201600%E2%80%93221%20BC.,China%20era%20from%201949%20until%20the%20present%20day, accessed on April 20, 2020.

14. Ibid.

15. n. 3.

16. Ibid.

17. Ibid.

18. "Emperor Taizong of Tang", Wikipedia, https://en.m.wikipedia.org/wiki/Emperor_Taizong_of_Tang, accessed on April 20, 2020.

19. Dennis C. Twitchett, "Taizong: Emperor of Tang Dynasty", Encyclopaedia Britannica, https://www.britannica.com/biography/Taizong-emperor-of-Tang-Dynasty#ref7081, accessed on April 21, 2020

20. Emily Mark, "Wu Zetian", Ancient History Encyclopaedia, https://www.ancient.eu/Wu_Zetian/, accessed on April 21, 2020.

21. Ibid.

22. "Confucianism", National Geography Resource Library, https://www.nationalgeographic.org/encyclopedia/confucianism/?utm_source=BibblioRCM_Row, accessed on January 10, 2021.

23. n. 3.

24. "Mongols in World History", Asia for Educators, Columbia University, http://afe. easia.columbia.edu/mongols/pop/,aps/images_maps.htm, accessed on January 11, 2021.

25. n. 3.

26. Paulette Cohn, "10 Facts about Marco Polo", Biography, https://www.biography. com/news/marco-polo-facts-netflix-series, accessed on January 15, 2021.

27. "Timeline of Chinese History", Wikipedia, https://en.wikipedia.org/wiki/ Timeline_of_Chinese_history, accessed on January 10, 2021.

28. "Ming dynasty", https://www.history.com/topics/ancient-china/ming-Dynasty, accessed on January 15, 2021.

29. Ibid.

30. n. 3.

31. Ibid.

32. "Opium Trade: British and Chinese History", Encyclopaedia Britannica, https:// www.britannica.com/topic/opium-trade, accessed on January 12, 2021.

33. Ibid.

34. Ibid.

35. n. 27.

36. "Boxer Rebellion", Wikipedia, https://en.wikipedia.org/wiki/Boxer_Rebellion, accessed on January 12, 2021.

37. Ibid.

38. "History of China", Wikipedia, https://en.wikipedia.org/wiki/History_of_ China#Qing_Dynasty_(AD_1644_%E2%80%93_1912), accessed on January 12, 2021.

39. "History of the Republic of China", Wikipedia, https://en.wikipedia.org/wiki/ History_of_the_Republic_of_China, accessed on January 12, 2021

40. "Chinese History—Republic of China 1911-1919", GlobalSecurity.org, https:// www.globalsecurity.org/military/world/china/history-republic.htm, accessed on January 12, 2021.

41. "Sun Yat-sen", Wikipedia, https://en.wikipedia.org/wiki/Sun_Yat-sen#Guangzhou_ militarist_government, accessed on January 12, 2021.

42. Ibid.

43. "The Republic of China (1912-1949)", https://totallyhistory.com/the-republic-of-china-1912-1949/, accessed on January 12, 20121.

44. Ibid.

45. n. 39.

46. Ibid.

47. Ibid.

48. Harold Tanner, "Chinese Civil War, 1945-1949", https://www.oxfordbibliographies. com/view/document/obo-9780199791279/obo-9780199791279-0031.xml, accessed on January 16, 2021.

49. "History of People's Republic of China (1949-1976), Wikipedia, https:// en.wikipedia.org/wiki/History_of_the_People%27s_Republic_of_China_ (1949%E2%80%931976), accessed on January 18, 2021.

50. Elizabeth C. Economy, *The Third Revolution* (Oxford University Press, 2018).

51. Ibid.

52. "The Great Leap Forward", Wikipedia, https://en.wikipedia.org/wiki/Great_Leap_ Forward#Industrialization, accessed on January 18, 2021.

53. Kallie Szczepanski, "Overview of the Chinese Cultural Revolution", ThoughtCo, August 25, 2020, https://www.thoughtco.com/what-was-the-cultural-revolution-195607, accessed on January 18, 2021.

54. Ibid.

55. Ibid.

56. "Cultural Revolution", Wikipedia, https://en.wikipedia.org/wiki/Cultural_ Revolution#Death_of_Mao_and_Arrest_of_the_Gang_of_Four_(Sept._1976), accessed on January 18, 2021.

57. Economy, n. 50.

58. Ezra F. Vogel, "China Under Deng Xiaoping's Leadership", East Asia Forum, https:// www.eastasiaforum.org/2011/09/27/china-under-deng-xiaopings-leadership/, accessed on January 19, 2021.

59. Britannica, T. Editors of Encyclopaedia, "Jiang Zemin," Encyclopaedia Britannica, August 13, 2020. https://www.britannica.com/biography/Jiang-Zemin, accessed on January 19, 2021.

60. "China under Hu Jintao", Facts and Details, http://factsanddetails.com/china/cat2/ sub7/item75.html, accessed on January 20, 2021.

61. David E. Sanger and Michael Wines, *New York Times*, January 16, 2011, as quoted in "China under Hu Jintao", Facts and Details, http://factsanddetails.com/china/ cat2/sub7/item75.html, accessed on January 20, 2021.

62. Ian Johnson and Keith Bradsher, *New York Times*, November 8, 2012, as quoted in "China under Hu Jintao", Facts and Details, http://factsanddetails.com/china/cat2/sub7/item75.html, accessed on January 20, 2021.

63. Xiaohuai Yang, "Xi Jinping: My Road into Politics", *Zhongua Ernu*, Interview from the summer of 2000 in the Chinese journal, translated by Carsten Boyer Thogersen and Susanne Posborg of Nordic Institute of Asian Studies, available on https://www.asiaportal.info/xi-jinping-my-road-into-politics/, accessed on October 17, 2020.

64. Michael D. Swaine, "China: The Influence of History", January 14, 2015, https://thediplomat.com/2015/01/china-the-influence-of-history/, accessed on April 14, 2020.

65. Ibid.

66. Johnson, n. 1.

3. China and its Foreign Relations

China—the People's Republic of China (PRC)—an aspiring superpower, also has aspirations of being the sole great power in the Asian continent. Its foreign policy is, hence, based on its strategic aims, along with the primary goals to preserve its independence, territorial integrity and sovereignty. Being a 'hyper-active' member of the international polity, it has full diplomatic relations with 178 out of the 193 UN member states, and it unswervingly claims that it follows an independent foreign policy in pursuit of peace. Any nation that does not recognise the 'One China' policy that the PRC is vocal about, that is, to consider Taiwan as a part of China, is considered hostile, and is excluded from direct interaction.

Being a member of the UN and as a permanent member of its Security Council (UNSC), and with its growing economy, China has the membership of numerous international bodies. The PRC replaced the ROC—Republic of China, commonly known as Taiwan—as a member of the UN in the early 1970s through a UN Resolution. Thereafter, it has signed various international agreements, including the Nuclear Non-Proliferation Treaty (NPT) in the UN, although it may not have followed them in letter and spirit.

The evolution of the foreign policy of any country is influenced by the history of its relationship with other countries, which then provides a framework for it to follow; so is the case with China. It is indeed necessary for all policy-makers of the many nations of the world to be conscious of Chinese history, for the Chinese themselves are extremely conscious of it. This chapter, therefore, would be an attempt to explain the evolution of China's foreign relations and why it does, what it does; the reader would well appreciate that it is well nigh impossible to enumerate and evaluate relations with each country! The legacy, in combination with China's economic progress, the rapid growth of its military strength, along with its ideology, have a bearing on its foreign policy, how it has behaved thus far and how it is behaving now, and what can be expected of it in the years to come!

Historical Legacy

Ever since the end of the Mao era and the subsequent opening up in 1978, Chinese leaders have been making frequent visits abroad, to countries in almost all regions of national interest to it, and seeking recognition for the country in various international forums and through regional treaties. However, there have been times when some aspects of its foreign policy formulation have been at odds with the official policies; what has been projected, till very recently, is that China's rise has been spoken about and portrayed as the growth of a developing nation, with world peace as the ultimate aim! As aforementioned, to understand the origin of, and the forces that have influenced, China's foreign policy, one has to flip back through the pages of its history; a quick look would then be in order.

China's relations with other countries, both within the neighbourhood and beyond, have been inspired by its long and rich heritage as one of world's oldest civilisations. It viewed itself as the undisputed cultural centre of the universe, with its uncontested supremacy and self-support, giving rise to the concept of the Middle Kingdom, with its emperor as the ruler of all mankind by virtue of his innate superiority and divinity; other countries, more so the vassal states in the immediate neighbourhood and near vicinity, hence, maintained deferential relations, rather than state-to-state relations as between equals. Consequent to this line of thought, China never really maintained any equivalent to a Ministry of Foreign Affairs; any country seeking trade with China was considered to be a tribute, or an offering to the emperor. The near neighbours were considered to be barbarians, although China, at times in its history, has been overrun by these barbarians, as during the Yuan and Qing Dynasties; nevertheless, these invasions were few, as the Chinese Army was frequently tasked with carrying out military expeditions to keep them at arm's length, and out of the country's borders.

With the succession of the Ming dynasty, after the downfall of the Mongol-led Yuan Dynasty, imperial China ventured overseas to project its power; Admiral Zheng He, a eunuch, as a representative of the emperor, led the 'treasure fleet' to Southeast Asia, through the Indian Ocean to the littoral states of East Africa, granting lavish gifts, but also collecting tribute to the Chinese emperor, even invading Sri Lanka, then known as Ceylon.[1] Although China had despatched diplomatic missions over land ever since the Han Dynasty (202BCE-220CE), these missions under Admiral Zheng were unprecedented in size and magnificence; between 1403 to 1419, 2,000 ships of varying sizes and utility, to service the seven different tribute missions that the emperor had planned, were constructed in Nanjing's shipyards.[2] Another interesting fact is that of the role played by eunuchs during this period. Going against the earlier policy of keeping the eunuchs uneducated and away from politics, as many as 75 eunuchs were placed in charge of foreign policy and they travelled frequently to the vassal states, and less frequently to far-flung areas, such as Japan and Nepal![3] Immediately after this, however, China went back to its isolationist policy, the *Haijin* or the sea ban, which restricted private maritime trading or the establishment of coastal trade posts; this continued till the early Qing Dynasty when it was strictly enforced, as against during the later years of the Ming dynasty when it comprised mere official proclamations.

There have been many periods in China's long history of it following isolationism. This was a practice that was followed by many a Chinese emperor, as above mentioned, due to a belief that China was the centre of civilisation, the empire was the Celestial Dynasty, the emperor was the leader of the civilised world, and the rest of the world was backward and poor with little to offer to China—a self-centred viewpoint indeed! Despite this self-centred viewpoint, China was also a centre of trade from early on in its past, from as early as the 2nd century BCE and continuing to almost the 18th century, with many of its commercial interactions coming from the Silk Route; some documented interactions are those with the Roman Empire in the third century BCE and the visits of Marco Polo between 1271 and 1295.[4] Marco Polo's accounts of his visits to China aroused the interest of the Western nations, leading to an increase in Western expeditions into Asia, mainly China, and, over the years, increased the apprehension of foreign imperialism. Britain, Spain, France, Holland, and Portugal, the main colonial powers, established colonies in Asia over the next three centuries;

Britain was a late arrival, and entered the continent through India, and later Singapore and Burma (now Myanmar).

During the Ming dynasty, China witnessed many upheavals in its foreign policy. As against the many durations of isolationism, there were also several periods of hardline Chinese foreign policy, examples of which are Admiral Zheng's tribute voyages; these are considered to be diplomatic high points of the period! Apart from the many maritime tribute missions of Admiral Zheng, China had extensive trade relations with the Portuguese and Spanish, who visited the Philippines at regular intervals and exchanged Chinese goods for silver. Silver was a commodity that was much in demand in China, so much so that Spanish-minted silver coins were commonly used during Ming China. The surplus of silver, together with wars and natural disasters, led to a decline in the Chinese demand of the commodity, leading to its devaluation and an adverse effect on the economy.[5] The soft power of the Ming dynasty was at the fore with visits of Jesuit missionaries, between the 16th and 17th centuries, who translated ancient classic Chinese texts into their own language, mainly Latin, and also exposed the Chinese to Western theses by translating them into the Chinese language.

As China opened its borders, many nations, whether regional, or from the West—primarily Europe—visited China to exchange ideas, religious or otherwise, or for commercial purposes. A series of border skirmishes with Russia occurred during the period 1652-1689, in which Russia was foiled in its efforts to occupy the land north of the river Amur; after the defeat of the Russians, the Treaty of Nerchinsk was signed between the emperor of China and the tsar of Russia in 1689, to delineate the borders between their two nations, some clauses of which exist till date.[6]

While maintaining cordial relations with the European countries to safeguard itself against their political and economic strengths, China, displayed no enthusiasm to appease the Western nations. As has been mentioned by Professor Kenneth Pomeranz in his book, *The Great Divergence*, China's economic infrastructure was far better than that of the European nations at the time.[7] It had the capability not only to meet the requirements of its many domestic markets, but also to meet the global needs; with its superior quality of life, met through adequate sanitation and a strong internal agricultural sector, China never really had any desire to satisfy the demands of the 'inferior' Western nations. As a result, China's perspective of the world did not undergo any major changes during the Qing Dynasty. It was only after the First and Second Opium Wars, that also began the era of unequal treaties, that changes occurred.

The demand, or what one could call the craving, for Chinese luxury goods, mainly consisting of fine porcelain, silk, and tea, the afternoon drink, for which the British, in particular, had developed a strong liking, increased many times over; to facilitate a quick turnover of goods, Britain established a trading post in Macau, in far Southeast China. Notwithstanding the fact that many ports were available for trade, the commercial preference of almost all the Western nations was to trade via Canton (Guangzhou), due to its geographical proximity to Southeast Asia. A licensing system was invoked, wherein a Chinese merchant firm, as an authorised agent, was issued a permit to trade with a Western ship, only at Canton, and it was the responsibility of the merchant to collect the taxes and deposit them into the government treasury; many restrictions were imposed, including prohibition on using other ports for trade, which were not very appreciated by the visiting ships, leading to smuggling, and bypassing of the legal system.[8]

What led to the Opium Wars? Britain, which had become the largest trading partner with China, imported British-made gold and silver jewellery, a demand for which had increased amongst the wealthy Chinese. As mentioned earlier, an unquenchable demand in Britain for Chinese tea and other luxury goods, caused a trade imbalance; the British had to pay with silver, as China was not interested in Western manufactured goods but demanded silver to mint its currency, having shifted from paper currency early in the Ming dynasty. By the mid-17th century, Japan's silver mines were all but depleted and Britain, along with other European nations and the New World nations, became the primary source for silver.

The widespread and strong influence of the global silver trade has been underscored by Adam Smith in his book *The Wealth of Nations*; while appreciating its market value, he was also captivated by the idea of how this commodity brought together the old and new worlds, namely, the West— America and the European nations— and China.[9] Under the Ming and Qing Dynasties, China had already understood the criticality of silver to the world economy and how it would contribute towards its own success in global commerce. China, therefore, amassed silver towards enhancing its trading power.

Silver continued to be the mainstay of trade in Europe through the 17th century and into the 18th century. The decrease in the supplies of silver caused difficulties for European traders to purchase highly desired luxury items from China. In the 19th century, American traders introduced opium into the Chinese markets as a medicine, which then turned to leisure consumption. As opium became popular, its demand soared, to the extent that Chinese traders soon began selling silver to fund their purchases of opium, rather than the other way around. Addiction to opium became the bane of China, leading to the Qing court seeking methods to end the trade. Severe restrictions were placed on the sale of opium, which led to rampant smuggling and widespread corruption amongst the officials. While the Europeans and Americans did not appreciate the restrictions, it was the British, who had by then established a near-monopoly through the East India Company, which decided to use military force to insist on compensations for the financial losses that had occurred. This led to a small confrontation between the British and Chinese naval ships in September 1839, followed by a full maritime engagement between the two countries in June 1840, wherein the Royal Navy bombarded the port of Dinghai with its superior ships and ordnance; this was the beginning of the First Opium War. After a series of decisive defeats at the hands of the Royal Navy, the First Opium War came to an end in 1842, with the Treaty of Nanking (Nanjing), which is considered by the Chinese as the first of the "unequal treaties".

Under the Treaty of Nanking that ended the First Opium War, China had to grant major concessions, both financially and territorially. China was made to pay a twenty-one million dollars compensation for the losses incurred by Britain, of which six million dollars was to be paid immediately and the balance in stipulated instalments; China was also forced to hand over control of Hong Kong island and the surrounding smaller islands, in permanence to Britain; it was also to permit trade from other ports in the northern parts of China, apart from Canton, in the southern seas, which was earlier the only port permitted for foreign trade; opium, however, continued to be contraband!

The Second Opium War (1856-1860), is referred to by many names; it is also known as the Second Anglo-Chinese War, the Second China War, the Arrow War, or the Anglo-French Expedition to China.[10] It was the second major war fought by the imperial European powers with the Qing Dynasty, over the export of opium to China. Notwithstanding the clauses of the Nanking Treaty, wherein Britain had been granted access to five ports, its accession of Hong Kong, the grant of an indemnity and extra-territoriality, Britain continued to be dissatisfied with China for not furthering trade and diplomatic relations.

In the period between the two wars, even as the Western powers continued to grow, both economically and gaining colonial territory, there were repeated acts of aggression against British subjects in China. Russia, France and America were the other nations that had a notable presence in China in the 1850s and had managed to further their territorial, trade and diplomatic interests through treaties signed in 1844.[11] The concessions and privileges that they had managed to squeeze out of China—primarily, a renegotiation of the treaties after 12 years—were now demanded by Britain with a renegotiation on the Treaty of Nanking; in the new demands, Britain mainly wanted facilitation of trade by British merchants, legalisation of the opium trade, exemption from taxes on British imports and residential permission for a British ambassador. The British, in an effort to circumvent the stringent trade and taxation rules then existing in China, offered Chinese merchant ships registration under the British flag, from Hong Kong. In October 1856, one such ship, *The Arrow*, (hence, the name 'Arrow War') flying a British flag, was boarded by Chinese marines on suspicion of piracy and 12 of the 14 Chinese crew members were arrested. Britain's demand for the immediate release of the crew and an apology for the insult to the flag, was met partially through the release of just a few of the crew members; later in the month, Canton was bombarded by a British warship, leading to skirmishes between Chinese and British troops, and a ceasing of trade. In December, British warehouses in Canton were set ablaze by the Chinese, leading to a further straining of relations.[12]

In early 1856, a French missionary was executed by the local Chinese authorities in the interior of China, for violating an entry ban into the region. This prompted the French to get into a joint battle with the British against the Chinese. In late 1857, additional British troops were made available after quelling a rebellion in India, and an alliance was formed between Britain and France, which moved ahead in victory and maintained control of Canton for nearly four years. USA and Russia offered support to the alliance; although Russia did not send any military forces, it did send an envoy; and despite the US government's promise of neutrality, a US warship participated in assistance to the alliance.[13]

The Treaties of Tianjin were signed in June 1858, marking an end to the first part of the war; four treaties that were signed by the alliance, which now included Russia and America too, opened 11 more ports for trade by the Western countries. Other salient features of the treaties were: these nations would be permitted to establish embassies in Peking (now Beijing), which until then was a closed city; all foreign ships would be permitted to sail on the Yangtze river; foreigners would be permitted to travel inland; China was to pay a compensation of about 200,000 kg of silver to Britain and half that to France; the terms of the treaties, although grudgingly agreed to by the Chinese, were, however, not ratified by the emperor's court. Prior to the Treaties of Tianjin, a separate treaty was signed in May 1858 between Russia and China, known as the Treaty of Aigun, which revised the border as had been determined through the Treaty of Nerchinsk in 1689, giving Russia control over the southern bank of the Amur river.[14]

Between 1858 and 1860, the alliance and China fought many battles; this period also marked the second phase of the ensuing Opium War, which ended in October 1860 with the signing of the Convention of Peking. These battles were severe and the Chinese suffered at the hands of the superior Western militaries; the Qing Army, although much larger in numbers, was overwhelmed and routed during the siege of Peking during which the palaces of the emperor, who had fled the city, were looted and burnt. The Convention of Peking that followed the defeat, imposed further territorial, financial, and penal restrictions on China:

- China had to ratify the Treaty of Tianjin signed in 1842 and open Tianjin as a trade port.
- The district of Kowloon, adjacent to Hong Kong, was also ceded to Britain.
- The financial compensation awarded by the earlier treaty was increased, with France now entitled to a similar amount as Britain.

- The opium trade was legalised.
- The embassies of Britain, France, and Russia were permitted in Peking.

"Beyond a doubt, by 1860, the ancient civilisation that was China had been thoroughly defeated and humiliated by the West."[15] Taking full advantage of the defeat, two weeks after the signing of the Peking Convention, Russia forced China to sign a 'supplementary' that forced it to cede the coastal region east of the Amur river to Russia; it was here that Russia then established the port city of Vladivostok. These three treaties, namely, the Treaty of Nanking, the Tianjin Treaty and the Peking Convention, are considered to be "unequal treaties" and have played on the minds of China's rulers ever since.

Accepting Western superiority, China, immediately thereafter, started a "Self-Strengthening Movement"[16], a period of institutional reforms spread over thirty odd years to modernise its administrative and political institutions, import Western military technology, impart professional military education, update its scientific knowledge with Western ideas, and build its shipping industry, along with telegraph and railways. The most important goal of this Movement was to develop the military industry, with the construction of military arsenals and ship-building yards to strengthen the navy; apart from the development of the military industry, schools for teaching mechanical skills and navigation were also established at these arsenals and dockyards. The reforms can be divided into three phases: Phase I (1861-1872); Phase II (1872-1885); and Phase III (1885-1895). There were, however, sceptics amongst the ruling elite and intellectuals who continued to believe in the old Confucian way of life and the traditional values of ancient China, believing that the agenda was limited to just economic and military modernisation. This, coupled with the territorial crisis with Russia (1881) and the Sino-French War (1885) waned the enthusiasm of pursuing the military reforms and shifted the focus, instead, to other industries, mainly the textile industry. The Movement did revive the Qing Dynasty from the verge of extinction, but the drive came to an abrupt end with China's defeat against the Japanese in the first Sino-Japanese War in 1895. The defeat also indicated the failure of the Qing Dynasty's "Self-Strengthening Movement" that had been initiated to modernise and strengthen its military with Western aid, Japan having acquired the expertise and equipment to outclass the Chinese as early as 1863.[17] The Sino-Japanese War was fought mainly in the Korean peninsula, and inflicted further ignominy to the Qing Dynasty with the loss of Korea, a tributary state; the defeat also ignited an unexpected and widespread hue and cry amongst the public, leading to a series of political uprisings led by Sun Yat-sen, which ended with the Republican Revolution of 1911 and the establishment of the Republic of China.

Opinion is divided amongst historians and scholars who think that the reforms were a failure, or that they had limited success; some, such as Michael Gasster perceived the Movement as inadequate due to the influence of conservative Confucian ideology, while others such as Luke S.K. Kwong feel that it succeeded in the spread of Western thought in industry, building of academies, overseas education and military education; yet another group with historian Immanuel C.Y. Hsu, thinks that the entire effort was a superficial attempt to modernise Chinese society, with no attempt to imbibe Western culture or philosophy.[18] Notwithstanding the debate on the success or failure of the reforms, as aforementioned, the Self-Strengthening Movement did revive the Qing Dynasty, which ruled China until 1911, and then with a brief revival in 1917, laying the foundation for modern China.

The term 'century of humiliation', associated with the rise of nationalism in China in the early 20th century, covers the period between 1839 and 1949, when the Chinese Empire was repeatedly defeated by the Western powers and Japan; this term is used repeatedly, even till date, as a reminder to the people of the humiliation suffered by China at the hands of the imperial Western powers and Japan. Nationalism was on the rise after the defeat of China in the first Sino-Japanese War, but the term arose in 1915, when, during World War I, Japan placed on the table, before China, a set of 21 demands; the demands, if accepted in toto, would have effectively made China a protectorate of Japan, a condition that was unacceptable, not just to China, but also to Britain and USA, which took umbrage at Japan's overbearing and bullying attitude![19] After strong and aggressive diplomacy by Britain, a whittled down list of 13 demands was placed before China, with a deadline of two days for acceptance, which was met by China, albeit with reluctance.

A widespread effect of the acceptance of the 13 demands by China was that it created ill-will towards Japan amongst the Chinese people, who retaliated by a boycott of all Japanese goods; although the boycott of the goods was just one effect, there was an extensive outpour of nationalist feelings amongst the people, which contributed significantly towards the subsequent students' movements. World War I came to an end with the signing of the Treaty of Versailles; signed in June 1919, it was followed by the Paris Peace Conference that, apart from stipulating the punitive damages against the losing nations, also gave control of the Shandong province of China to Japan, much to China's disappointment.[20]

The loss of Shandong, and the lack of recognition of China's status as a sovereign state, despite it having joined the winning side in the war effort, placed a deep-rooted mistrust of the Western nations in the minds of even the common citizens. This manifested in the students' demonstrations, popularly known as the May Fourth Movement of 1919, and in many subsequent demonstrations; the sentiment has been exploited over generations by successive governments to their advantage. In the long time that has passed after the signing of the Treaty of Versailles, China has shown tremendous transformation, politically, materially, and in its military; the early leaders of the Republic of China, first established in 1911, would probably be surprised to see how the People's Republic of China, that followed on the culmination of the civil war in 1949, has become so powerful in all spheres. These changes, and the power that it has garnered, does not, however, mean that the legacy of China's 19th century period after the Opium Wars, and the post-Versailles era, has been disregarded. In fact, it is the other way around; the unpleasant memories of China's woes at the hands of foreign powers have continued to be a source of Chinese nationalistic sentiment since 1949.

Viewing foreign powers always with a shadow of doubt, opposition to even a hint of an inferior status, and desire to reassert sovereignty and independence have strongly influenced the Chinese foreign policy. The rejuvenation and revival of the Chinese nation has, therefore, been paramount in the minds of the rulers of China and the leaders of the Communist Party; this was manifested in the announcement by the present-day ruler, Xi Jinping, immediately after his taking over as president.[21] It is not that the revival did not matter much to his predecessors, but Xi Jinping, as compared to those before him, has made it his mission, working relentlessly towards achieving the lost status and avenging the century of humiliation. The trials and tribulations of attempting to remove the unequal status that China found itself burdened with in the comity of nations, has often influenced its behaviour in international politics; the present-day resurgence has not really modified China's perceptions of the world order of the 20th century, something that it wishes to modify in perpetuity, for the 21st century.

Foreign Relations : Republican China

The imperial era, it can be said, came to an end in China in 1911, when the imperial court was overthrown by the Republican Revolution; but it also brought about an era of confusion. Yuan Shikai, a military and government official, who rose to power towards the end of the Qing Dynasty, garnered support from the regional warlords, to make an attempt to establish himself as a dictator.[22] Not much interested in establishing relations with other nations, except for obtaining loans from the European countries, he laid the foundation of his autocracy with a modern army and bureaucratic control, and was declared as the first president of the Republic of China in 1912; his sudden death in 1916, left a void and the country in a state of chaos; with hardly a central government worth its name in Beijing, warring regional warlords ruled almost the entire nation.

With World War I raging in Europe, China too pitched in, playing a small role. Japan, on the other hand, also a part of the Allied forces with Britain, seized all German-occupied territories in China; in 1915, Japan issued the Twenty-One Demands[23]. As above-mentioned, the demands, which were followed by the Treaty of Versailles and the Paris Accord, permitted Japan to retain the territories, but, in the bargain, Japan lost the trust of Britain and USA; there was also a rise of hostile nationalism against Japan in China.

Regional warlords, who ruled the roost in almost all of China, did not have any interest in foreign affairs; the small legacy establishment in Beijing, working as the central government, had little or no control over most of China, but it did control foreign affairs and was so recognised by other nations. The central government of China negotiated for an increase in its share of the customs revenue, and also represented the country in international parleys, as in the Paris Peace Conference; it also made a bid to bargain against the terms of the unequal treaties, though not with much success.

Germany had lost its occupied territories in Republican China when Japan seized them in 1914. Being the loser in World War I, Germany, in the Treaty of Versailles, was again at the losing end, with territorial and fiscal penalties. Yet, the German military had a major role to play in Republican China, providing advisory services and training of the Chinese Army; almost all training academies and army units in China had embedded German officers and other personnel.[24] Apart from the help from the German military, engineers and bankers provided their services and loans for the Chinese railroad system. Trade with Germany flourished in the 1920s, with Germany as the largest supplier of government credit, until Nazi Germany aligned itself with imperial Japan—China's greatest enemy! The last of the German advisers left the country in 1938; nevertheless, the German template for growth, development and the organisation of the army, continued to be used by Chiang Kai-shek through the civil war and the Sino-Japanese War (1937-1945).[25]

During the early 20th century, China's desire for sovereignty and Japan's growing ambition for playing a major role in Asia for access to labour, food and raw materials, resulted in a clash of interests; Japan invaded China in July 1938, resulting in a long-drawn and brutal war, which also turned out to be the biggest war of World War II in Asia. China, at that time, had aligned with the Allied powers and by 1938, had USA as its strong supporter. Michael Schaller, as quoted in Wikipedia says:

> China emerged as something of a symbol of American-sponsored resistance to Japanese aggression.... A new policy appeared, one predicated on the maintenance of a pro-American China which might be a bulwark against Japan. The United States hoped to use China as the weapon with which to contain Tokyo's larger imperialism.[26]

Republican China, while fighting its internal civil war against the Communists, did, however, unitedly fight Japan for eight long years; yet its contribution as the first Allied power to fight an Axis power in Asia, thwarting Japan's imperialistic ambitions, is not discussed much in military history. If China had not put up a strong front against Japan in 1937, the course of the war in Asia could possibly have been different! China also played an important role in halting the Japanese advance in Burma (now Myanmar) and helping secure the Stilwell Road between Northeast India and Lashio (Burma). Yet, its military contribution towards the war effort of the Allied powers in Asia in the longest of all battles, has neither been well documented nor publicised, as some of the other battles fought by the Allies, such as the Battle of Midway of the Americans, or that fought at Kursk and Stalingrad by the Russians, or the Battle of El Alamein of the British; another sore point for China of unequal treatment![27]

At the end of World War II, China stood out as a nation with a fairly strong military, but it was also a nation with a collapsed economy, drained of its resources, with the people disgruntled with the growing corruption and miseries brought about by natural disasters; it was also a nation on the brink of an all-out civil war between the Nationalist Kuomintang Party (KMT) led by Chiang Kai-shek and the Communist Party (CPC), led by Mao Tse-tung, that broke out soon thereafter and ended only in 1949.

China's civil war that continued with military gains and losses on both sides was closely monitored by USA and Soviet Union, neither of which offered any military aid, but did make unsuccessful attempts to get the warring factions together to form a coalition government. The civil war continued through to 1949, with the Communists making steady gains in occupying a major portion of the country; the end of the war was a foregone conclusion for the KMT. On October 1, 1949, Mao Tse-tung announced the establishment of the People's Republic of China (PRC), from his capital at Peking, with small pockets of resistance by the KMT continuing till the end of 1949. In place of Chiang Kai-shek, who had, now, fled and established the Republic of China (ROC) in Taiwan, stood Mao Tse-tung and his triumphant Communists.

Foreign Relations: People's Republic of China

China's size, its huge population, natural resources, growing military strength, and sense of history placed it, initially, in the unusual position to decide how self-reliant or dependent on others it should be in order to modernise;

a continual quandary that the Chinese policy-makers have faced since the 19th century. As this policy fluctuated, Chinese foreign relations have alternated between a tendency toward isolation (self-reliance) and periods of openness to foreign assistance and influence. The dichotomy that exists between China's actual capabilities since 1949, and its perceived potential, has been another salient and distinctive feature of its foreign relations of being seen as a developing country, also often wanting to be treated as a major global/regional power, with special relationships with the United States, Russia (erstwhile Soviet Union), Japan and other smaller nations in its neighbourhood.

The Chinese foreign policy, since 1949, has been affected by its physical size, the size of its population, historical legacy, worldview, nationalism, and the ideologies of Marxism-Leninism and Mao. Combining with China's economic growth, and decision to grow militarily, these factors have had a fluctuating influence on its governmental structure, feelings of nationalism for territorial integrity and reunification, and display of sovereignty.

Historical legacy has, at times, led China towards isolationism, a tendency to avoid international involvement, primarily due to a general mistrust of foreign powers and the sufferings inflicted upon the Chinese people by them; the century of humiliation has never been forgotten by its leaders, and neither have they let its people forget it; this, in fact, had been the only common thread between Mao's Communist Army and Chiang Kai-shek's nationalist army! There have always been outbursts of nationalist sentiment, either with demonstrations, or statements, against any foreign power, even at the slightest implication of China being an inferior nation; Mao's statement in 1949, after the establishment of the PRC that "the Chinese people have stood up"[28] and Deng Xiaoping's statement in 1982, on the issue of arms sales to Taiwan, that "no country can expect China to be its vassal or expect it to swallow any bitter fruit detrimental to its interests",[29] are just some examples of leaders keeping the fire of nationalism burning in the hearts of the people.

Chiang Kai-shek and his KMT Army were pushed into Taiwan after their defeat on the mainland; it was here that the 'Republic of China' (ROC) was formed in 1949, with the PRC functioning on the mainland. The ROC continued to announce itself as the genuine claimant of being the Chinese nation for four decades thereafter; notwithstanding, immediately upon its establishment, the PRC was recognised by the Eastern Bloc nations, followed by the United Kingdom and Switzerland in January 1950, and Sweden in the very next month; Sweden was the first Western nation to establish diplomatic ties with the PRC in May 1950.[30]

As a great power with aspirations of being a superpower, China's foreign policy and strategic thinking are closely interlinked. While the basic objectives of the foreign policy are quite the same as those of any other nation, such as the maintenance of territorial integrity and the creation of a favourable international environment for its own growth, China has not earned the trust of many a nation due to its actions and utterances.

Closely linked with the strong feeling of nationalism is the desire to restore to itself, areas that were earlier carved out by the imperialist Western powers, Russia, and Japan, for serving their respective interests. Restoration and preservation of territorial integrity and sovereignty are two major foreign policy goals of China. The control established by the Qing Dynasty over Outer Mongolia (present-day Mongolia), had lapsed long before 1949, and had been replaced initially by Tsarist Russian, and then a Soviet influence; China's recognition of Mongolia, hence, as a separate nation in 1949, most likely would have been with great hesitancy and disappointment at not being able to re-establish its control over it. Nevertheless, this was not the case with Tibet, to which China attaches great strategic importance; military force was used in 1950 to occupy it, and then later in 1959, to strengthen its occupation. Use of force since 1959, has been a regular feature to ensure the continued suppression of the Tibetan people. Tibet is the bone of contention between the PRC and India, since the Dalai Lama was provided shelter in India in 1959, and has also been permitted to establish a government-in-exile in India, much to China's chagrin.

Two other territorial issues that are linked with Chinese history are Hong Kong and Macau, areas that were ceded to Britain and Portugal respectively after the 'unequal' treaties of the late 19th century that were forced upon China; both these territories were handed over to China in 1997 and 1999, after negotiations in the mid-1980s, under an agreement of 'one nation two systems', which were to give both Hong Kong and Macau greater autonomy as special administrative regions of China. What conditions and restrictions prevail there today is a different story! Nonetheless, the return of these regions to sovereign China is considered to be a great diplomatic victory; for China, Taiwan is a pending thorny issue for reunification, achievement of which is paramount, no matter what the cost—even by using military force and while doing so, may be even confronting American military might, which may come to Taiwan's aid! With the legacy of mistrust between the KMT and the CCP, a peaceful solution does not seem to be on the horizon!

Many Western countries continued to maintain diplomatic relations with the ROC in Taiwan until late 1970, with the ROC even occupying the allotted seat for China in the UN Security Council (UNSC). It was only in 1971, after the PRC was recognised as the legitimate claimant for the seat in the UNSC, that the ROC was expelled and many nations switched their diplomatic relations from Taiwan to Beijing. The controversy of two self-governing countries, the PRC and the ROC that started with the end of the Chinese civil war, continues till date, with many countries maintaining only a 'trade and cultural relationship' with Taiwan, and only a handful maintaining full diplomatic relations.

Another salient feature of China's foreign policy is the influence of ideology, both Marxist-Leninist and Maoism, wherein it is believed that conflict, not necessarily military, is inevitable, be it between imperialism and socialism, or between classes within a nation. Opposition to imperialism, what China perceived as foreign powers' hegemony, constituted an important part of China's foreign policy, which further led to nationalism. In a simplified definition, it may be said that China had focussed on USA's rise during the 1950s just after the victory in World War II, on opposition to the Soviet-style of socialism in the 1960s, and on opposition to the dominance of either superpower thereafter. During this process, it continued to attempt the spread of its own style of socialism and feelings of anti-colonialism, through encouraging revolutions in newly-independent countries. China probably took its inspiration from Lin Biao's famous 1965 essay, "Long Live the Victory of People's War" and covertly promoted rebellions in Indonesia and quite a few African nations, many of which later broke off diplomatic relations with China.[31] China's image of a revolutionary country that wanted to support local Communist Parties in other nations, more so in the surrounding regions of Asia, continued to grow through the 1970s to the

1980s; it was then that it realised the adverse effects of such a stand on its relationship with others.

While never swaying from its principles that have guided the formulation of its foreign policy, China's leaders, since 1949, have amended their stand on stratagems as per their understanding of the international geopolitics and their own aims. This may appear to be a contradiction, but it does adhere to one of Mao's many statements: "We should be firm in principle; we should also have all flexibility permissible and necessary for carrying out our principles."[32] As per its leaders, China has always laid out long-term goals for itself without being influenced by other nations, no matter how severe the provocation may be; as a result of which pronouncements in its policy documents contain strong definitive words such as "always" and "never".[33]

An example of China's display of continuity in its foreign policy, since 1949, is the constitution of the "Five Principles of Peaceful Coexistence", and their inclusion in treaties that China signed with many a nation, being first included in an agreement with India in 1954. China used these five principles to its advantage in the mid-1950s, when it looked to nurture a bonding with newly independent countries in Africa and Asia that had broken away from the shackles of imperialism and colonialism, just as China had done earlier. However, within a few years, when the Cultural Revolution was well under way in China, the relationships turned sour, to the extent that many of the countries broke off diplomatic relations with China. With the end of the Mao era, and changes in leadership in the CCP, the Five Principles gained prominence once again to be formally included in the Constitution of the CCP in 1982, and were thence considered as the foundation of all future relationships with any nation.[34]

Comprehension of the 'why and how' of the foreign policy of any nation can be a major study in itself. To understand the foreign policy of a country like China, so steeped in secrecy, the who, why and how about decisions was, therefore, a major task, until the end of the 1980s decade. The opaqueness of the structure of foreign-policy-related decisions was removed by Deng Xiaoping, after the Mao-Zhou Enlai times; he also initiated steps to institutionalise the decision-making process, in an effort to make it less personality-based, although the process, it seems, has not been fully completed!

With the passage of time, as its relationship with the rest of the world stabilised, China streamlined its foreign policy too, with other nations coming to know the who's-who in the decision-making loop, and which ministry/ organisation was to be contacted for the job in hand; nevertheless, the CCP Secretariat and the State Council, together carried the joint responsibility for major decisions. China shed its image of isolationism and opened to the world, with the leadership, down the hierarchy, travelling abroad and meeting their respective counterparts to ratify or abrogate agreements, but with the approval of the State Council and Secretariat.

From a state of disarray and confusion in 1949, through the Cultural Revolution and the decades thereafter, China emerged as a contemporary power, aspiring for its perceived rightful place in the world, that of standing abreast USA and may be, ahead of Russia. It has been seeking a higher profile in the UNO, based on its permanent—veto-power—seat, and the membership of many international economic organisations. In its immediate neighbourhood, China has been making attempts to reduce bilateral tensions by stabilising relations and resolving border and other contentious issues; this became more noticeable towards the end of the 20th century and moving onto the 21st century. China's foreign policy, can, thus, be summarised as strategic relations, both regional and international, to create a favourable environment to further its national interests.

China's Foreign Relations in the 21st Century

At the turn of the century, in 2005, China, which had already established relations with the Association of Southeast Asian Nations (ASEAN), held an inaugural session of the East Asia Summit (EAS), with the ASEAN+3— India, New Zealand and Australia. Earlier in July 2001, it signed a Friendship Treaty with Russia, as a follow-up to the improvement of ties between the leaders of the two nations, Jiang Zemin and Vladimir Putin; these two nations joined hands with the Central Asian countries—Kazakhstan, Kyrgyzstan, Tajikistan, and Uzbekistan—to set up a new group, the Shanghai Cooperation Organisation (SCO), to promote stability and fight terrorism within the region. In September 2006, during the UN session, Brazil, Russia, India, and China, combined as the four major emerging economies to form a group with the acronym BRIC (South Africa joined later in 2011 to form BRICS); although the group has an agenda of conducting bilateral relations amongst the members based on non-interference, mutual benefit and equality, there are multiple economic, political and territorial disputes among the five nations!

In the last decade of the 20th century and early 21st century, it so appeared that China wished to improve relations with Russia and Europe, as a balance to the sole superpower, USA. However, after the Kosovo War and discussions within the CCP think-tanks, a need was felt in the echelons of the policy-makers to reorient the foreign policy to cater for a unipolar world; a new concept was articulated to manoeuvre in the post-Cold War era through diplomatic and economic alliances, rather than the earlier mindset of the Cold War of competitive and hostile coalitions. This was propagated to the world as 'China's peaceful rise'. The new concept influenced China's relations with ASEAN, the formation of the SCO and BRICS, as well as cooperation with USA to contain North Korea's missile and nuclear proliferation; nevertheless, China's continued opposition to the nomination of its two major neighbours—India and Japan—to the UNSC, as permanent members, has proved that it will brook no competition against itself in its rise as a regional power and an important role player in the world!

The then general secretary of the CCP, Hu Jintao, had spoken to a Party audience in August 2004, wherein he specified that China would continue to follow an "independent foreign policy of peaceful development, while maintaining a peaceful and stable environment among China's neighbours."[35] Such statements by the Chinese leadership have not changed since 1949, however, the style, brusque or mellow, has been adapted to the prevailing domestic and international political situation. In a Foreign Ministry statement in 2007, China issued an eight-point clarification on the philosophy of its foreign relations wherein it re-emphasised the above, as well as reiterated the Five Principles of Coexistence as had been pronounced by Zhou Enlai; in addition, catering to the existing situation in the world, it opposed terrorism and proliferation of Weapons of Mass Destruction (WMD).[36] Such pronouncements, with some additions and deletions, as per the personality of the then leaders, have been made at regular intervals thereafter, until the aggressive policy of Xi Jinping, broadcast after his taking over the reins in 2012.

As earlier mentioned, at the heart of Xi Jinping's vision, as was expressed by him during his first press conference on being appointed as the general secretary of the CCP in 2012, was his call to the Party cadre and the general population for the rejuvenation of the Chinese nation.[37] This depiction is well understood in China as it projects a nationalist population with assertive leaders at the helm; not included in the narrative, nonetheless deeply etched in the memory of the people, are the periods of national shame and humiliation inflicted upon China by the colonial powers, and periods of embarrassment and dishonour from contemporary history, such as during the Cultural Revolution and the Tiananmen Square massacre. Nevertheless, in moving ahead to accomplish the process of rejuvenation, Xi Jinping has projected an image of a strong China, poised to take on the world with its own value system and political structure. In this, China has shed its low-profile foreign policy as was initiated by Deng Xiaoping, and instead adopted bold steps while vying for global supremacy. The display of an aggressive style, and a hithertofore not seen belligerence, has been termed as 'wolf-warrior' diplomacy, a term based on Chinese action films of the same name, wherein its diplomats, spread all over the world, strongly denounce any criticism of the country.[38]

The strident wolf-warrior diplomacy commenced when, around 2010, China overtook Japan as world's second-largest economy. In a display of confidence on the world stage, the foreign policy became more forceful, probably an indication of the current Chinese leadership of Xi Jinping abandoning Deng's guideline of 'keep a low profile, bide your time', which in the Chinese lexicon of diplomacy is also known as *taoguang yanghui*.[39] The new style of diplomacy is evident not only in words but also in actions; in early April 2020, China sank a Vietnamese fishing trawler in the South China Sea (SCS), near the disputed Paracel Islands, claiming that the trawler was engaged in illegal activities in Chinese waters; in March 2021, more than 200 Chinese fishing boats and subversive Chinese militia parked themselves well within the Exclusive Economic Zone (EEZ) of the Philippines in the SCS, refusing to move out and claiming to be within China's territorial waters. In the opinion of the Chinese government, wolf-warrior diplomacy is nothing but an effort to set straight records that had been botched up by the biased-Western media and the wrong interpretations thereafter. China's image suffered greatly after the outbreak and the late reporting of the COVID-19 virus, leading to a worldwide pandemic; it has been seen as a cover-up of its shortfalls in not just the reporting, but also in controlling the spread. The calls from the international community for access to its laboratories, especially the Wuhan laboratory, for detecting the source of the virus, have been consistently either denied or ignored, leading the other nations to believe that it has something to hide.

Wolf-warrior diplomatic engagements have often triggered strong responses and backfired against some of China's diplomats and institutions. In early 2020, China took umbrage to a narrative in an American newspaper, the *Wall Street Journal*, leading to a tit-for-tat expulsion of journalists from both sides. While the hawks in China's diplomatic corps continued their rhetoric and display of their aggressiveness, there were some mellowed voices too; senior veteran diplomats have opined that China should uphold "the spirit of humility and tolerance, and adherence to communication, learning, and openness".[40]

Bearing in mind the growing negative image of China, and an increasing worldwide clamour for independent investigations into the origin and spread of the pandemic, Xi Jinping, seems to have taken a softer stand. In a speech to the CCP's top leadership, he asked the country's confrontational official media and the wolf-warrior diplomats, to present the country as a "credible, lovable, and respectable China". Instead of an aggressive tone, Xi wants the Party's propaganda machine to send out a message to the world that all that China wants is "the Chinese people's happiness and good fortune".[41] That Xi Jinping wants a shift to portray a positive perception of the country, is evident from his statements, nevertheless, any alteration in the policy, cannot comprise mere words in a speech, and has to be translated into action. It is apparent, however, that China has realised that its bullying demeanour is raising the costs for it and making it easy for the Western nations to push it into a corner.

The shift from maintaining a low profile in international affairs to one that is seen today, is a part of Xi Jinping's drive towards rejuvenation of China. As a display of economic and military might, China has established and constructed, while ignoring international objections and apprehensions, forward military bases in a few of the small islands in the SCS; it has also operationalised a military station, purportedly a logistics base, in Djibouti (Djibouti also has bases of USA, Italy, France and Japan), raising concerns about its intentions. Through its Belt and Road Initiative (BRI), China has managed to acquire a significant involvement via investments, in strategic ports in Europe and Asia, causing much alarm to other regional nations. China has also made efforts to portray itself as a leader in addressing global challenges, such as global warming and associated climate change; using its clout as the second-largest economy, it has recommended new trade and security institutions, while objecting to any efforts by other nations to counter its proposals, or form new alliances without including it!

Another important aspect of China's diplomacy, quite different from its show of aggression, is the use of soft power. Interest in the use of soft power was aroused in Chinese officials as far back as the early 1990s, when a book authored by Joseph Nye on the subject was translated and discussed by Chinese scholars and analysts. It was not, however, adopted as official diplomatic practice until 2007, when Hu Jintao connected Chinese rejuvenation with the use of soft power; much of Xi Jinping's use of soft power is a follow-up from what his predecessor had started: providing grants to developing nations, promoting Chinese language and culture through a vast, worldwide network of more than 500 government-funded Confucius Institutes, positioning media outlets in critical foreign markets, and actively supporting Chinese think-tanks to interact with their counterparts in other nations. Then again, there have been instances when the soft power has not been so soft; some Western university faculties have opposed Chinese diktats, such as not to host the Dalai Lama. In some cases, such opposition has led to the closure of the Confucius Institute, as in University of Chicago.[42]

In Conclusion

There is no doubt that Xi Jinping has established himself as the core leader and 'president for life' in China, having removed the two-tenure restrictions on the presidency through changes in the Constitution. China's future aims, or rather Xi Jinping's thinking for the future, of being a power parallel to USA in the world order, does not seem to be moving ahead as per his plans on a smooth road, neither in the BRI, nor on the foreign relations front, or even otherwise.

All nations, when moving in the narrow passage of international relations, want to portray a positive image of themselves as friendly, and wanting to increase their circle of influence to improve international public opinion. So does China. It was Xi Jinping who deviated from Deng Xiaoping's strategy to keep a low international profile. This translated into an aggressive foreign policy, reacting strongly when its interests were under threat; this has resulted in losing 'friends', some of whom even wanted to remain on the right side of China. A Pew poll released on April 21, 2021, indicates a negative view of China in USA, UK, Germany, and Canada[43]; the EU, which wanted to maintain cordial relations with China, has also changed its stance. China's assertive posturing has affected relations within East and Southeast Asia; the Philippines, which, after winning its case on maritime claims in the SCS, had been wanting to get closer to China, is now having second thoughts. China's portrayal of itself as expansionist is not just for territorial gains, but to present itself as the 'next superpower in waiting'; its policies seem to be designed to transform the existing global order to reflect its own image. This is resulting in a 'us vs them' 21st century Cold War!

The belligerent posturing, and display of effrontery that was briefed to its diplomats in a show of strength may have been very religiously followed by them, but has not yielded favourable results as was probably desired. The argumentative and confrontational diplomats of the wolf-warrior policy may have won, but Chinese diplomacy has definitely not! Developments in June 2021 are an indication that even Xi Jinping has realised the need for a mellowed down foreign policy—an unprecedented admission, may be indirect, of failure of the earlier policy, coming from an autocratic core leader of China!

Will China really overhaul its foreign policy in an effort to improve its relations with other countries, or will it just tweak the existing policy, and continue with some cosmetic changes?

Only time can tell.

Notes

1. "Foreign Relations of Imperial China", Wikipedia, https://en.wikipedia.org/wiki/Foreign_relations_of_imperial_China, accessed on April, 10, 2021.
2. Ibid.

3. Ibid.

4. Ibid.

5. Dennis O. Flynn and Arturo Giraldez, "Cycles of Silver: Global Economic Unity through the mid-Eighteenth Century", *Journal of World History*, 13, no. 2, Fall 2002; excerpts quoted in "China and Europe 1500-2000 and Beyond: What is Modern", https://afe.easia.columbia.edu, accessed on April 10, 2021.

6. "Treaty of Nerchinsk", Wikipedia, https://en.wikipedia.org/wiki/Foreign_relations_of_imperial_China and https://en.wikipedia.org/wiki/Treaty_of_Nerchinsk, accessed on April 10 2021.

7. Kenneth Pomeranz, *The Great Divergence* (Princeton University Press, 2000), https://archive.org/details/greatdivergence0000unse, accessed on April 10, 2021.

8. "Canton System", Britannica, https://www.britannica.com/event/Canton-system, accessed on April 15, 2021.

9. "Global Silver Trade from the 16th to 19th Centuries", Wikipedia, https://en.wikipedia.org/wiki/Global_silver_trade_from_the_16th_to_19th_centuries#China_and_the_demand_for_silver, accessed on April 15, 2021.

10. "Second Opium War", Wikipedia, https://en.wikipedia.org/wiki/Second_Opium_War, accessed on April 15, 2021.

11. Kenneth Pletcher, "Opium Wars", Britannica, https://www.britannica.com/topic/Opium-Wars, accessed on April 15, 2021.

12. n. 8.

13. Ibid.

14. Ibid.

15. Immanuel C. Y. Hsü, *The Rise of Modern China* (New York: Oxford University Press, 2000), as quoted in"Second Opium War", Wikipedia, https://en.wikipedia.org/wiki/Second_Opium_War, accessed on April 15, 2021.

16. "Self-Strengthening Movement", Wikipedia, https://en.wikipedia.org/wiki/Self-Strengthening_Movement, accessed on April 17, 2021.

17. "Meiji Restoration", Wikipedia, https://en.wikipedia.org/wiki/Meiji_Restoration, accessed on April 17, 2021.

18. Hsü, n. 15.

19. "Twenty-One Demands", Wikipedia, https://en.wikipedia.org/wiki/Twenty-One_Demands, accessed on April 17, 2021.

20. "Treaty of Versailles", Wikipedia, https://en.wikipedia.org/wiki/Treaty_of_Versailles, accessed on April 17, 2021.

21. Elizabeth C. Economy, *The Third Revolution* (Oxford University Press, 2018), p. 3.

22. Wikipedia, "Yuan Shikai", https://en.wikipedia.org/wiki/Yuan_Shikai, and https://en.wikipedia.org/wiki/History_of_foreign_relations_of_China, accessed on April 20, 2021.

23. n. 19.

24. Wikipedia, https://en.wikipedia.org/wiki/History_of_foreign_relations_of_China#Republican_China, accessed on April 20, 2021.

25. Ibid.

26. Ibid.

27. "What was China's Role in WW II?" https://www.worldatlas.com/articles/what-was-china-s-role-in-wwii.html, accessed on April 22, 2021.

28. University of Southern California, Annenberg, US-China Institute, "The Chinese People have Stood Up! 1949", Title of the opening address, delivered on September 21, 1949, by Mao Tse-Tung, at the First Plenary session of the Chinese People's Political Consultative Conference, https://china.usc.edu/Mao-declares-founding-of-peoples-republic-of-china-chinese-people-have-stood-up, accessed on April 25 2021.

29. Christopher S. Wren, "New Charter Due for Chinese Party", *New York Times*, September 2, 1982, https://www.nytimes.com/1982/09/02/world/new-charter-due-for-chinese-party.html, accessed on April 25, 2021.

30. Wikipedia, "History of Foreign Relations of China", https://en.wikipedia.org/wiki/History_of_foreign_relations_of_China, accessed on April 25, 2021.

31. Wikipedia, "History of Foreign Relations of the People's Republic of China', https://en.m.wikipedia.org/wiki/History_of_foreign_relations_of_the_People%27s_Republic_of_China, accessed on April 30, 2021.

32. "The Influence of Ideology", Country Studies—China, U.S. Library of Congress, http://countrystudies.us/china/125.htm, accessed on April 30, 2021.

33. Ibid.

34. Ibid.

35. Wikipedia, "Foreign Relations of China", https://en.wikipedia.org/wiki/Foreign_relations_of_China", accessed on April 25, 2021.

36. "Beijing Likens Cheney Criticism to Nosy Neighbour", *The Washington Times*, March 1, 2007, https://www.washingtontimes.com/news/2007/mar/01/20070301-104826-2978r/, accessed on April 25, 2021.

37. Economy, n. 21.

38. Air Mshl Dhiraj Kukreja, "China's Wolf-Warrior Diplomacy", *Defence and Security Alert*, Web edition, June 4, 2020.

39. Zhiqun Zhu, "Interpreting China's Wolf-Warrior Diplomacy", *The Diplomat*, May 15, 2020, https://thediplomat.com/2020/05/interpreting-chinas-wolf-warrior-diplomacy/, accessed on May 16, 2020.

40. Ibid.

41. Harsh V Pant, "Is China Backtracking on its Wolf-Warrior Diplomatic Style?", Op-ed, *Hindustan Times*, June 14, 2021.

42. Elizabeth Redden, "Chicago to Close Confucius Institute", Inside Higher ED, September 26, 2014, https://www.insidehighered.com/news/2014/09/26/chicago-severs-ties-chinese-government-funded-confucius-institute, accessed on June 14, 2021.

Note: Confucius Institutes are Chinese government funded language and cultural centres. The network of more than 1,700 institutes and classrooms worldwide is funded through grants from China, and they are usually on university campuses. The Education Ministry of the Chinese government, co-joined with the CCP, is responsible for overseeing the activities of these institutes.

43. J.J Moncus and Laura Silver, "China—PEW Poll", PEW Research Centre, https://www.pewresearch.org/fact-tank/2021/04/12, accessed on June 14, 2021.

4.   A Reset in China-India Ties

History

China and India have had historical relations as two great and ancient civilisations with similarities in culture, way of life and religion. Ancient India influenced China through the spread of Buddhism and ancient China influenced India through trade. Very many of us, in our childhood, would have read about Hieun Tsang, now known as Xuanzang in Mandarin, the Chinese Buddhist monk and scholar, who travelled to India between 627-643 AD, a long 16 years, covering almost the entire northern belt from Peshawar, then in undivided Hindustan, to, what is now, Bangladesh. During his stay in India, he studied ancient Buddhist scriptures, translating them from Sanskrit to Mandarin, and interacted with Buddhist monks and royalty, notably, King Harsha Vardhana. Although he was not the first, the narrative of his visit to India—The Great Tang Records on the Western Regions—written on his return home, forms a major source of information on Indian civilisation during those times[1].

The Silk Route was the major trade highway that helped establish cultural and economic ties between China and India in the early days. Subsequently, during the times of British rule in the 19th century, opium export by the British East India Company was the mainstay of trade with China, which later triggered the two Opium Wars between the Qing Dynasty and Britain and France between 1839-1860. Contemporary China still holds a grudge against the Western powers, especially Britain, for the crushing defeats and humiliating concessions granted thereafter in trade, with surrender of territory. During World War II, British India and China, fighting under the common banner of the US Command of the China-Burma-India theatre, played an important role in stopping the march of Imperial Japan that was causing untold chaos and destruction in its ruthless invasions in East and Southeast Asia.

Despite this close interaction between the two countries there has not really been a friendly understanding of each other after gaining independence. While India gained its independence from Britain in 1947, China came under Communist rule in 1949; the Chinese Communist Party (CCP), under Chairman Mao Zedong (Mao Tse-Tung), pushed the Nationalist Party, Kuomintang (KMT), fighting under Chiang Kai-shek, into Taiwan and formed the People's Republic of China (PRC) on the mainland. The modern relationship between China and India, which began in 1950, has swung from unabashed love, *Hindi Chini Bhai Bhai*, to deep suspicion, as in 2020. It was in 1950 that India, among the first to do so, terminated its ties with the Republic of China (ROC), now based in Taiwan, and recognised the PRC as the legitimate government of Mainland China. It was also in 1950 that China's occupation of Tibet sowed the seeds of suspicion, more so when the Dalai Lama sought refuge in India in 1959, and has been here since then. China's occupation of Tibet removed the buffer that earlier existed between India and China, and brought it as its next-door neighbour.

China itself underscores Tibet as the central issue with India by laying claim to Indian territories on the basis of Tibet's spiritual connection, rather than any acknowledged Han Chinese connection; indeed, ever since China annexed the historical buffer, it has laid claim over the entire Indian state of Arunachal Pradesh, terming it as Southern Tibet, a term it coined for itself as recently as around 2006! Of late, it has also been eyeing parts of northern Sikkim, over which it never raised any issues when Sikkim ceded to India in May 1975.

In the north, China continues to occupy about a fifth of the erstwhile state of Jammu and Kashmir (J&K), now split into the Union Territories of J&K and Ladakh. The area occupied by China is Aksai Chin, a huge, flat, salt desert at an altitude of about 5,000 m above sea level, with an area that covers about 37,244 sq km; it is a barren ground, which India's first Prime Minister, Jawaharlal Nehru, referred to as "an area where not a blade of grass grows", when informing the Parliament of the Chinese incursion! A brief history of the western and eastern borders that India inherited from the British would be in order here.

William Johnson, a civil servant with the Survey of India proposed the "Johnson Line" in 1865, which put Aksai Chin in Kashmir[2]. At that time, China did not control most of the Xinjiang region, as a result of which this line was never proposed to the Chinese, but only to the Tibetans. The line was to link Demchok in the South with the 18,000 ft high Karakorum pass in the North, taking a roundabout route beyond the Kun Lun mountains, and hence, included the barren and cold Aksai Chin desert within Kashmir. The Indian case for ownership of Aksai Chin rests essentially on the cartographic expeditions of Johnson, but no efforts were made to either define the border on a map or to establish any posts on the ground to secure the area. Historians, of the period of Lord Curzon in India during the early 1900s, have a long story to tell of how the Russians wanted to expand southwards towards India, eyeing a warm-water port, and how lines were drawn by empire-builders, sitting in the comfort of their armchairs in faraway England with their group of secret agents, cartographers, commercial travellers and explorers, to either protect territory through incursions, or plan expansions. Events of the beginning of the 20th century are of significance; the Russian Empire had weakened, first defeated in 1905 by a modernised and rising Japan, and then by the slow and steady rise of the revolutionary forces, which finally culminated in the Russian Revolution of 1917. Around the same time, China was also witnessing a change; the decadent Qing emperor was overthrown and the ROC came into being under the nationalist Kuomintang, with the rise of Communism alongside. To cut a long story short, with the exit of the British from India, and the collapse of the Russian Empire, it was China and India that inherited the dirty, and at times bloody, squabbles along the undefined or ill-defined borders!

The British, when they departed from India, left behind maps that showed several lines; one of the lines was running along the Kun Lun mountains, which is referred to as the Johnson-Ardagh Line and shows Aksai Chin as territory within Jammu and Kashmir (J&K). Another such line is marked closer to the Karakorum range, described as the Macartney-MacDonald Line, and yet another line is called the Foreign Office Line.[3] After 1947, it was left to the claimants, such as the rulers of J&K, Tibet, and the Indian and Chinese governments to decipher and resolve!

China-India Disagreements

It was through this region of Aksai Chin that the Chinese built a military road between 1951 and 1957, later christened as Highway 219; about 180 kms pass through the disputed area of Aksai Chin and connect Lhasa in Tibet with Karghilik in Xinjiang (also known as Yecheng in Chinese, it is a town about 250 kms southeast of Kashgar).[4] The Indian administration had no clue about it, and it was objected to by India only in 1957, well after it had been completed! The Chinese idea of defending these inhospitable mountainous areas is to keep the Indian forces well away, at a distance from this strategic road, now fully paved since 2013.[5] This development was the centre of border disagreements, which led to clashes between the two countries in 1962, after which China has continued to retain physical control of the territory in Aksai Chin and administer it as its own. The area remains a bone of contention between the two countries till date. Despite this region being uninhabitable and having no resources, it is strategically important for China, as it connects Tibet and Xinjiang with the rest of the country. It was this area that was the focal point of the violent clashes in May-June 2020, since China now wants to push the Indian forces further westward to cater for increased artillery and surveillance ranges, and safety for the military stations that have now been built.

The eastern boundary too is not without its share of debate and divergence of perception. In October 1913, the British called for a conference at Simla (now Shimla) and invited Tibet and China to attend; while the Tibetan authorities attended eagerly, being in conflict with their Chinese rulers, China was a reluctant attendee. Henry McMahon, then foreign secretary to the 'Government of India' and considered an expert at demarcating boundaries with the experience of drawing the Durand Line at the northwest frontier two years earlier, led the British delegation. What followed is the now famous McMahon Line, which extended the limits of British India up to the edge of the Tibetan plateau.[6] Although there was not much clarity for the cartographers, it was an ethnic non-Tibetan boundary, except for the Tawang constituency. As can be expected of such meetings, where all attendees are not in unanimous agreement, the Chinese, although having signed the agreement, albeit with reluctance, soon renounced the Simla Convention, and hence, by default, also the McMahon Line. While the British government never challenged the Chinese suzerainty over Tibet, it, also, never did make the McMahon Line effective as the border until 1937, when the Survey of India, for the first time, showed it as the official boundary.[7] After the Survey of India markings of the official boundary, there was confusion all around in the recognition of it, since China had earlier repudiated the Simla Convention. In 1938, brushing aside objections by Tibet, the Survey of India published a map; around the same time, the British government also made a precautionary move to proclaim sovereignty over Tawang, by sending a small military column under Capt GS Lightfoot to the area[8]. However, it was not until the Japanese advance towards India in World War II that the British moved with a sense of urgency to fix this boundary firmly and securely. The British then, in 1944, established their administration in the entire belt, with several posts of the Assam Rifles; soon after, Tibetan government officials were also packed off from the Tawang tract. Overriding the Chinese and Tibetan protests, the Indian government established itself firmly in the Tawang tract in 1951.

The British left India in 1947, and two years later, in 1949, the Communists came to power in what came to be known as the People's Republic of China (PRC). Shortly thereafter, China announced its intentions to move its army into Tibet; India's protests notwithstanding, China occupied Tibet in 1950, stating that "Tibet is an integral part of China and the problem of Tibet is a domestic problem of China. The Chinese People's Liberation Army (PLA) must enter Tibet, liberate the Tibetan people and defend the frontiers of China".[9] The bait offered to the PRC by India to desist its advance in Tibet, of recommending a membership of the UN in place of the ROC, now established in Taiwan, was rejected as an absurd quid pro quo![10]

The question that, therefore, arises is : why did India not claim, and subsequently exercise its control over the borders it claimed in the western and northern sectors as it did in the East? If the geography of the two regions is examined, the answer would become obvious. The topography in the eastern sector is totally different from that in the western and northern sectors, although it is the same Great Himalayan range of mountains that runs all along the border; the highest mountains in the East are generally about 12,000-15,000 ft, whereas in the western and northern sectors, the average elevation, especially in the area of contention, is about 16,000 ft and above. The boundary claimed, lies beyond two high mountain ranges and is logistically and militarily hard to defend. Besides, the Chinese were already in control of much of the area by 1951!

It can, thus, be seen that haphazard, historical records, differing perceptions of the border on the ground, and the machinations of cunning political leaders have left behind these lines, purportedly marking the borders, to be deciphered by 'experts' from both sides, although unsuccessfully!

Inherited Disputes Continue to Simmer

A further question that then arises is : why did India not make serious diplomatic or military efforts to claim control over territories that it so firmly believed were Indian? The Chinese, in their perception, had occupied territory, give or take a few sq km, within their claim line in Ladakh, which went further westward of the many lines that had been drawn by the Johnsons, Macartneys and MacDonalds. Apart from this, in the thinking of the then Indian leadership, the barren, uninhabitable, windswept, and desolated piece of land in the high mountainous terrain, was not worth the military and economic efforts that laying claim to it would demand. This was, despite the fact that newly independent nations of that period defended their inherited boundaries zealously, and considered them as sacrosanct, often without regard to geography, ethnicity and history.

The friction in the India–China relations had begun. The two governments decided to keep a lid on the problems while competing for advantages in other domains. On the surface it was all *Hindi Chini Bhai Bhai* and the practise of the *Panchsheel* philosophy of peaceful coexistence, while beneath the surface was the awareness that the claiming rights to large expanses of territory under the control of both nations were under dispute. The lid on this simmering cauldron was blown away when the Dalai Lama fled to India in March 1959 and was granted political asylum, much against the wishes of the Chinese.

India's domestic politics was also at play. India claimed what the Chinese were claiming and what they were occupying was our 'sacred land'; this was accepted by almost all, except the doctrinaire Marxist Communists of India, who may have done this for reasons not really related to history. There were some other incidents that occurred in 1959, which had an impact on the affairs of border management by the political leadership, in addition to partisan politics rearing its ugly head (it is important to mention this here, though details are being omitted). Suffice it to say that the influence of the domestic necessities in the international politics of democratic countries must never be underestimated! There is an inherent feature in democratic societies, wherein policy-makers, at times, have very limited flexibility in making a choice from a wide spectrum of options. Partisan politics, just as it is now playing a role in the moulding of the India-China relations, played an extremely important role even then.

In the years since the debacle of 1962, little has changed in India in so far as politics is considered; crucial security issues in India are still not able to get together a non-partisan consensus! The real and futile nature of the border dispute with China does not seem to have been comprehended as yet. While it may have been possible for India to settle its eastern border dispute with China on the basis of a demarcated McMahon Line, but now, considering the existing conditions since 2020, even that seems improbable. Given Xi Jinping's ambitions of the Belt and Road Initiative (BRI), there also seems absolutely no prospect of persuading China to hand over Aksai Chin back to India, for that would then de-link Tibet from Xinjiang, an almost sure strategic no-no, besides the loss of face for China in the world and the domestic audience. Can India then repossess it from China by military means? Even if India summons the political will to invest a fortune to wage a war, the question is debatable! To add to India's concerns, Pakistan has ceded to China a part of occupied J&K-Pakistan Occupied Kashmir (POK); under what is known as the "Sino-Pakistan Boundary Agreement" signed between China and Pakistan on March 2, 1963, Pakistan illegally ceded 5,180 sq km of Indian territory in POK to China.[11]

What Next

It can, thus, be seen that the seeds of the boundary dispute between China and India have a historical background and emerged when the PRC occupied Tibet. The numerous Confidence Building Measures (CBM), agreed upon through the years, during meetings at various levels, and the formal and informal talks between the current political leadership of the two nations, have not really helped in building mutual trust. There are two main reasons for the tension along the Line of Actual Control (LAC), as the India-China border is known: one, the differing perception of where the LAC actually runs, as it is neither marked on the maps accurately nor marked on the ground; a thick line drawn on the map can cover a few 100 m on the ground! The Indian perception of the international border is the Johnson Line, which China has rejected outright; for India, the LAC runs along what was occupied by it in 1959, while China's perception of the LAC is much further west, where it had reached during the 1962 conflict. The other reason is the build-up of infrastructure by China close to the border and in Tibet. China has a head-start against India, having begun the construction of a road-rail network and military bases and airfields, some two decades ago, across the entire Tibetan plateau. India, on the other hand, has accelerated the infrastructure development only in the last few years; the clash in May-June 2020 was over an objection to a road that connects Leh to the Karakoram pass. China definitely would not want India to threaten its transportation network or military bases! The unresolved border, which China farcically calls the LAC—Line of Actual Control—(with emphasis on *ACTUAL*) and has been reluctant to resolve, arms it with a leverage to keep India under military pressure, and, hence, under economic strain.

In the absence of a recognised border, neither clearly delineated on maps, nor demarcated on the ground, how, then, is border management carried out? The management of the India-China border is governed by the Peace and Tranquillity Agreement (PTA), 1993, and the Confidence Building Measures (CBM) Treaty, 1996. Further additions to this framework have been incorporated with time, in 2005, 2012 and 2013. These treaties accord recognition to the LAC and include not just the differing perceptions of both countries, but also the fact that the establishment and recognition of the border is still work in progress.

Kiran Rijiju, former minister of state for home, reported in Parliament that between 2010 and 2014, there had been a total of 1,612 transgressions on the LAC.[12] Most violations are not reported in the media. While violations on the LAC are commonplace, there are also two to three incidents each year involving a more serious confrontation. In April-May 2020, Chinese and Indian troops were involved in two non-lethal but aggressive actions in Ladakh and Sikkim, which followed a pattern. Immediately after these, was a brutal attack on Indian soldiers, leading to the loss of many lives in Ladakh—the first in the last 45 years—which, though it did not involve the use of firearms, yet were serious enough to alarm the world and get India prepared for a long military standoff against China.

The greatest challenge, therefore, for India is the resolution of the border dispute. With 2012 marking the fiftieth anniversary of the Sino-Indian conflict, old memories were revived, not that the memories were ever erased; this, coupled with a now-off-now-on show of belligerence by China towards its claim on Arunachal Pradesh, dubbed as South Tibet in Chinese parlance, and the most recent incursion in the Aksai Chin region of Ladakh, India, is, not in the least, likely to accept any Chinese overtures. China needs to redefine its actions in establishing its claim to Indian territories, just as it needs to put to rest the fears amongst the smaller nations in the South and East China Seas, which are opposing China's claims in these waters.

China-India Economic Options

Another aspect of the bilateral relations is China's most insidious warfare against India in the economic realm. India realises it, yet it has done little to avoid providing raw material to the Chinese economy, which, in turn, has been undermining Indian manufacturing through dumping of cheap products—television sets, furniture, toys, and even statuettes of Indian Gods, and many other products! Although the recent events of 2020 have marginally reduced the trade imbalance and the current account deficit, the earlier imbalance with China has been a major contributor to India's economic woes. Prolonging such a skewed economic relationship gives China little incentive to bridge the political divide; it, in fact, serves China's strategy to prevent India's rise as a peer competitor.

China is Asia's largest economy and the world's second-biggest with a GDP of about US$ 13.6 trillion; in comparison, India stands at number three in Asia, at US$ 2.7 trillion.[13] China is India's biggest trading partner, next to USA, a position that USA occupied till 2019; it supplies industrial components and raw materials to investments in India's start-ups and technology firms, chalking up more than 14 per cent of India's imports.

In return China accounts for a little more than 5 per cent of India's total exports, which translates into a huge trade deficit for India. India's imports from China have jumped over 45 times since the turn of the century, to reach over US$ 70 billion in 2018-2019.[14]

"India has to review and reduce this trade deficit, or in other words, economic dependence on China", the veteran diplomat, Gopalaswami Parthasarthy, wrote in the Hindu Business Line.[15]After the violent clashes of June 2020 in Aksai Chin, Ladakh, and the call by Prime Minister Modi to become "*atmanirbhar*"—self-reliant—economic nationalism has taken an upswing in India. As many as 59 mobile phone applications, with another 40 odd related applications, have been either banned or restricted; Foreign Direct Investment (FDI) from countries with a 'common land frontier' (read China) is to be scrutinised before acceptance, making China appear as the biggest loser. Earlier, in November 2019, India, at the last moment—just a day before the meeting in Beijing—refused to join the Regional Comprehensive Economic Package (RCEP), a trade bloc proposed by China that would bind other major Asian economies to it; a refusal that has irked China no end! India, previously had not joined China's BRI proposals in South Asia, and had also expressed reservations in international forums, discouraging some South Asian neighbours, again much to China's annoyance.

A study done by economists at the Sorbonne in 2008, on the late 20th century conflicts, had concluded that while openness to trade does not automatically prevent war, there is a greater risk for conflict when countries grow less economically dependent on each other, as appears now happening in the case of China and India.[16] Ironically, it means that globalisation can make matters worse as a country (India) that integrates itself into the world economy, can withstand the loss of economic interaction with a single nearby rival (China). Another example of a flashpoint within Asia is the Korean peninsula, where the trade between the two Koreas is almost zero, with an omnipresent risk of a major conflict. Closer home is the case study of India's most thorny link with Pakistan; after gaining independence, nearly a quarter of Pakistan's exports came to India, while about 50 per cent of its imports were from India. This cross-border trade slowly dwindled through the 1950s until the 1965 War when, for almost a decade, trade stopped, and then never really recovered as in earlier times. India, today, considers countries like Nigeria, Belgium and Mexico as larger export partners than Pakistan, a country with a long shared-border.[17]

While experts think, and even some Indian political leaders have said so in the past, that there is no major reason for rivalry between China and India, it is each to its own style. China does not shy away from mixing politics and business. It has a record of covertly or overtly using trade to punish countries, which do not acquiesce to its opinions and methods. For example, Japanese exports to China sank 13.2 per cent in just the first seven months of 2012, when China began wielding the trade sword as soon as the dispute over Senkaku Islands flared up[18]. In 2020, with the pandemic raging in the world, China has been threatening many nations with such trade sanctions, which have 'dared' to raise their voices against its handling of the pandemic, like Australia and Britain, to name a few. India, too, is in its crosshairs and is thus, being drawn into the US' circle of influence in response to the rise of a more assertive and aggressive China.

Xi Jinping had proclaimed, when announcing his project of 'One Belt One Road'(OBOR), which was later changed to the BRI, that China wishes to see the world live in harmony; what was left unsaid, but implied, was that China would be at the helm in such a world. All nations are on edge because of the calamity that they are facing, both societal and economic, which is testing not just human resilience, but also the political and economic manoeuvring of nations. And yet, some nations are behaving as if it is business as usual, continuing to pursue outstanding differences, unresolved issues, old grievances, and rivalries, in the race towards global leadership or regional supremacy, following a path of bias and intolerance, while pursuing their own narrow ambitions for developing their spheres of influence, instead of interdependence. Sadly, USA and China, the leading economies of the world, have also succumbed to such actions, which only compounds the tragedy because "grown-up nations are supposed to behave like grown-ups".[19] The ensuing upheaval has led to divergence of actions, rather than convergence, with attacks and counter-attacks.

India-China Diplomatic Options

India and China, both Asian giants, have an intricate relationship, which, with an exasperating frequency is fraught with recurring pushes-and-pulls, misgivings, and issues that have defied resolution, leading to continuous mistrust, notwithstanding all the positive statements that capture media headlines when the current leaders of the two countries meet, informally or formally. The year 2020 commemorated 70 years of the establishment of diplomatic relations between the two countries and was to be used to resolve pending issues, as was decided in the meeting between President Xi Jinping and Prime Minister Modi at Mamallapuram (erstwhile Mahabalipuram) when they met in October 2019. Yet, while efforts to control a raging pandemic continue, the PLA is up to its offensive activities confronting the Indian Army along the shared, but undemarcated, borders.

In such a scenario, can China-India ties be reset to the benefit of both countries? In so far as the handling of the pandemic is concerned, China could definitely have done better. The WHO was not informed in time; the doctors who raised an early alarm were persecuted; other nations and international organisations, like the UN, could also have been informed well in time. China, in an attempt to placate the world opinion, offered to donate diagnosis kits and Personal Protection Equipment (PPE), which was later found to be defective and returned to China; to make matters worse, Chinese companies then made efforts to sell the defective PPE to some other countries. India had initially offered help to China, but as relations slipped downhill, and China's reputation too took a hit, India's assistance also stopped. This was followed by the military deployment of the PLA in Sikkim and eastern Ladakh, leading to the incursions and skirmishes, and the loss of lives on both sides.

Amid the rush of nationalistic fervour in India, generated by the military action in Ladakh, there is little indication that cooler heads will prevail as of now. On the other hand, it needs to be remembered that after the 2017 confrontation at Doklam that lasted 73 days, diplomatic relations were never reversed; if anything, the relations between the two leaders, Xi and Modi, saw a new bonhomie develop, probably because the two saw the need of a consensus to further deepen their economic and social links.

On the economic front, China needs to appreciate how much it will benefit with India's growth, just as the prosperous Western nations gained from it becoming rich in the last two decades. It would have been better for China to audit its Belt and Road Initiative projects in Nepal, Bangladesh,

Sri Lanka, and Myanmar, rather than leave India with the feeling of being threateningly encircled by a "String of Pearls"; what India is going through now, is quite like NATO's expansion into Eastern Europe in the 1990s after the USSR break-up, leading to a lasting mistrust between USA and Russia.

Whatever course of action India or China may follow to reset ties, neither country will compromise on its national interests. India's reaction to China's intrusions has been on all three fronts—economic, diplomatic, and military—and all driven by national interests. On the economic front, while India has barred the participation of Chinese companies in strategic domains such as information technology and communications, it cannot place similar restrictions in other areas. Indian companies are dependent on China for raw materials and other intermediary products and cannot switch off the supply chains overnight. Similarly, the restrictions on Chinese investments in Indian companies should not be seen with a biased view.

Chanakya, the great philosopher of ancient India, is reported to have advised his king that "your immediate neighbour is your natural enemy, as he covets your territory and resources, and is positioned to take them, if he is more powerful than you".[20] India has always considered China as more powerful than itself and viewed it as a threat, but never really expressed it in such terms; there have been only two defence ministers, George Fernandes and Mulayam Singh Yadav, who clearly saw China as the main threat and did not hesitate in saying so.[21] The many prime ministers of the country, from Nehru to Modi, have made efforts through direct interaction with the Chinese leadership to move the relations ahead and have extended a hand of friendship, realising that while the issue of the border remains unresolved, economic ties are of greater importance. Hence, the diplomatic push!

For the diplomatic push to be successful, India has, for long, been cautious of joining any anti-China bloc, with its fears and inhibitions also preventing it from taking any unilateral step. To retune its ties with China for the future, India would have to rearrange its foreign policy and reset its entire geopolitical posture, blending it with an economic policy towards China. During the period of the pandemic, China's economy has been affected as much as those of the other nations of the region and the world. India should tie up with international organisations to take advantage of the situation. More trade barriers against China could be placed on the table to make it difficult for it to export manufactured goods, if it does not mend its ways; after all, China's economy is more export driven, and the global demand for its products has fallen greatly!

Diplomatically, India should take care that it does not fall into the US trap to contain China, while moving ahead with closer interaction with regional allies like Vietnam, Philippines, Indonesia and Taiwan and Australia and Japan. India's partners in East and Southeast Asia are equally mindful of China's growing assertiveness and aggression, for their sovereignty is threatened by Xi Jinping's autocratic hunger for power. Another trap that India should be wary of is that of China's sweet talk. English language newspapers for the international audience mention that the Chinese Ministry of Foreign Affairs and Ministry of Defence are keen on re-establishing peace and tranquillity; the prevailing view in China, on the other hand, as mentioned in Mandarin newspapers, emphasises India as having reversed the status quo in the region through its "turbocharged diplomatic opportunism and military adventurism".[22] For China, India was, is, and will remain, an economic, political, and military competitor.

China questions India on its non-alignment status, considering its pronounced tilt towards USA as a threat to its own ambition to rise as the sole superpower, thus, negating the possibility of a strong India-China relationship. China, hence, wants to thwart India-US ties under the US' Indo-Pacific vision, while building its own ties with India, but definitely not at the cost of its sovereignty and territorial integrity. It is looking at a new world order post-pandemic, with itself at the helm, especially when the world has seen the American reaction in countering the pandemic's spread in the country, and also in the world. As aforementioned, China too, is in a vulnerable position for its initial handling of the pandemic and faced an intense backlash; to counter the adverse reactions amongst all countries, barring a few, China resorted to aggressiveness through its 'wolf-warrior' diplomacy[23], projecting a muscular stance against not just India, but many other nations too.

The Future

If a degree of normality in the India-China relationship has to be built, it will have to be upon the foundation of bilateral relations between the two countries thus far. The meetings of 2018 and 2019 between the leaders of China and India that generated the 'Spirit of Wuhan' from China, and carried it forward to Mamallapuram in India, were held to reduce friction; but somewhere the friction has aggravated with patriotic emotions in both nations, hindering the chances of a mutually-agreed upon conciliation. A settlement of diplomatic and nationalist impulses, both involving a certain amount of give-and-take, will prove to be a challenge for leaders in both countries.

Does China really want to alienate India, or even vice versa? If China was to cede the disputed territory, it would lose face, both at home and internationally; it may even have to agree to more Indian demands, and may be even from other nations, both options totally unpalatable to an ambitious leader like Xi Jinping! India, on the other hand, wants to maintain cordial relations, notwithstanding China's uncooperative and obstinate stand vis-à-vis sponsored-terrorism from Pakistan in J&K, and its obstruction against India gaining membership of the Nuclear Suppliers Group (NSG) and the UN Security Council (UNSC).

Can then, the relations between India and China see an upswing through arbitration by a third party? Again, it depends on which is the third party. China sees India as unreliable with the growing closeness between USA and India, while it goes through a sustained trade war with USA and its allies. Could Russia play the role of a responsible mediator? Russia did not intervene during the Doklam standoff between China and India in 2017. However, during the 2020 standoff in Aksai Chin, Russia did get the foreign ministers of India and China together in a virtual meet during the raging pandemic; the Russian foreign minister, however, stated that Russia would not arbitrate in the border dispute, since India and China have bilaterally resolved disputes in the past, and would likely do so now as well. The three countries have existing partnerships and growing cooperation; in addition, Russia and China have a common antagonism towards USA. India's partnership with Russia, therefore, should ease China's concerns about India's trustworthiness, while India has learnt to segregate its relations with Russia and China while ignoring their relationship with Pakistan.

Whatever course of action India adopts, as mentioned earlier, there can be no appeasement expected from it. It could use its leverages against

China, giving a strong indication that two can play the game. Engagement with the Association of Southeast Asian Nations (ASEAN), Taiwan, Japan, Australia, and the immediate neighbours of South Asia, could necessarily become more of a permanent nature, without appearing to be a regional bully or a hegemon; with these actions, India may also espouse a hard line view-point on Tibet, which is actually the Achilles heel of China.

The future could be built on an objective relationship between India and China, as mutually responsible countries that work for a world order which would be inclusive, open, compassionate, development-oriented, and which respects diversity and the rule of international law. India has played its cards well thus far, even prior to the onset of the pandemic. Considering the existing circumstances for China, India can be expected to mobilise international opinion, but it must do so strategically and not with an emotional viewpoint. India has to display its strengths and Chanakya wisdom and, hence, defend itself.

Notwithstanding, the chances of reform in the India-China relations in the coming days, seem extremely remote.

Notes

1. "Xuanzang", Wikipedia, https://en.wikipedia.org/wiki/Xuanzang, accessed on June 15, 2020.
2. Mohan Guruswamy, "The Great India-China Game", June 23, 2003, https://www.rediff.com/news/2003/jun/20spec.htm, accessed on July 18, 2020.
3. Lt Gen PJS Pannu, "Defending a Historically Undefined Border Line", *Hindustan Times*, June 23, 2020.
4. "China National Highway 219", Wikipedia, https://en.wikipedia.org/wiki/China_National_Highway_219, accessed on June 17, 2020.
5. Ibid.
6. Guruswamy, n. 2.
7. Ibid.
8. "Tawang District", Wikipedia, https://en.wikipedia.org/wiki/Tawang_district#cite_ref-6, accessed on July 21, 2020.
9. Mohan Guruswamy, "The Battle for the Border", June 23, 2003, https://www.rediff.com/news/2003/jun/21spec.htm, accessed on July 21, 2020.
10. Ibid.

11. "Sixteenth Report of the Committee on External Affairs (2016-17) on Indo-Pak Relations", p. 12, available on https://eparlib.nic.in/bitstream/123456789/65278/1/16_External_Affairs_16.pdf, accessed on June 22, 2020.

12. Quoted by Maj Gen Moni Chandi, "A 73-Year-Long Intractable Border Dispute", Insights, May 2020, www.synergiafoundation.org, accessed on May 16, 2020.

13. Mahima Kapoor, "Six Things to Know About India-China Economic Relations", https://www.bloombergquint.com, June 19, 2020, accessed on June 23, 2020.

14. Ibid.

15. David Fickling, "The Most Troubling China-India Conflict is Economic", https://www.bloombergquint.com, June 18, 2020, accessed on June 23, 2020.

16. Ibid.

17. Ibid.

18. Brahma Chellaney, "Dancing in the Dragon's Jaws", *The Mint*, October 22, 2013.

19. Nirupama Rao, "India and China: Ancient Ties Need New Stimulus", *Insights*, www.synergiafoundation.org, accessed on May 17, 2020.

20. Shashi Shekhar, "India and China Clash, it's Time to Heed Chanakya", *Hindustan Times*, June 21, 2020.

21. Ibid.

22. "From Summitry to Standoff: What's Next for India-China Relations?", available on https://www.youtube.com/watch?v=kwguBjJmlkA, recap available on https://www.wilsoncenter.org/issue/great-power-competition, accessed on July 31, 2020.

23. Air Mshl Dhiraj Kukreja, "China's Wolf-Warrior Diplomacy", available on https://www.dsalert.org/chinas-wolf-warrior-diplomacy/, accessed on June 9, 2020.

5.   China: Xi Jinping at the Helm

An Overview

The arrival of China on the global stage, be it due to its economic reforms, its passive and aggressive diplomacy, or its domestic politics, has been accompanied by a plethora of information about the country on anything and everything, from the ratio of its ageing-to-working population, stock market fluctuations, to its domestic policies and the quirks of its leadership! Such information, whether online or available in print, achieves its purpose of keeping the world informed, or misinformed, on issues regarding one of the important powers of the world, namely, China.

Yet, the information, like all information, has the potential to overload the reader, and does create doubts about its veracity, more so if it is from the 'official Chinese sources or media' known for their obfuscating practices. For example, one day, one may read about the Chinese government's crackdown on illegal activities and on its promise of enforcing the rule of law and order, and the very next day, there would be reports of the arrest of over 200 lawyers and activists, without any due legal process or any plausible reason![1]

Nevertheless, there is one process that is sacrosanct in China, and that is the conduct of the sessions of the National Congress of the Communist Party of China (CPC), commonly cited as the Chinese Communist Party (CCP), every five years, during which members of the Politburo Standing Committee (PSC) and its leader, the general secretary, are elected and announced; these are then followed by the annual plenary sessions wherein major policies are announced. The election of the president follows about four months later during a session of the National People's Congress (NPC). In comparison to the US presidential elections or the Indian general elections, wherein the political and personal leanings of the public servants are announced and examined threadbare, the membership of the PSC is not privy to many and is almost totally behind closed doors; what goes on behind the closed doors is generally power-brokering—recommendations of erstwhile rulers and the examination of the popular personalities from amongst the members of the PSC.

It was one such selection process that had been initiated on November 8, 2012, a routine procedure, yet unique for many reasons: for the first time in the past two decades or so, the selection of the general secretary did not have the stamp of approval of Deng Xiaoping. Considered to be a visionary leader, Deng was influential in major CCP decisions from after his appointment in the wake of Mao's Cultural Revolution in the late 1970s, till even after relinquishing the prime post, and until his death in 1997. Each of the previous four general secretaries—Hu Yaobang, Zhao Ziyang, Jiang Zemin, and Hu Jintao—had his stamp of approval even when he was not at the helm himself. Without Deng now, the process appeared not only unclear, but also riddled with confusion: Bo Xilai, once strongly tipped for the top position, fell out of favour and was expelled from the CCP earlier in 2012, after allegedly being involved in bribery, embezzlement and abuse of office (the scandal also typified everything that was amiss within the CCP and the complete political environment in China); Xi Jinping, the heir-designate and the final choice, also had been out of public sight for about two weeks in September, giving rise to speculations on his fate too. It was only when the group of the elected seven members, as against the earlier nine of the PSC, walked into the Great Hall of the People in Beijing on November 15, 2012, that the veil of uncertainty was finally lifted, and the future leaders were made known to the people of China and the world; the 18th National Congress of the CCP had made its choices! Xi Jinping, at the young age of 59—the first general secretary to be born after the formation of the People's Republic of China—now occupied the ultimate position in the CCP as general secretary, with the other six elected members of the Central Committee; he was now on the threshold to take on the mantle of president of China after four months, along with other lead positions in various important committees, and yet, he was an unknown entity, even after his three-decade-long government service!

Xi Jinping: A Brief Life History

The young Xi Jinping spent his early childhood in relative luxury, his father, Xi Zhongxun being a deputy prime minister of China, and a close associate of Mao Zedong. The senior Xi, however, lost his exalted position in the Party and the government due to his frequent and open criticism of government actions, both before and during the Cultural Revolution. His father being branded as a traitor and consequently jailed for his bourgeois background, resulted in Xi Jinping himself, then a mere 15-year-old in 1969, being despatched to a remote village in rural Shanxi province and assigned to work as farm labour in an agricultural commune. During the six years that he worked as farm labour, Xi Jinping developed a good relationship with the peasantry, which would pay dividends later in his life and help in his rise through the Party ranks.

Notwithstanding his exile and his father falling out of favour with the CCP, Xi Jinping bore it no ill will, rather, he made several attempts to gain membership of the Party. In 1974, he was formally granted membership and initially served as a branch secretary. In 1975, when the then Prime Minister, Zhou Enlai, started the Four Modernisations covering agriculture, science, industry and military, to kick-start China's economy and revitalise the society, Xi Jinping's upward journey in the Party commenced with admission to a course in Chemical Engineering at Beijing's prestigious Tsinghua University, as a worker-peasant-soldier student.[2]

Xi's university education continued to be influenced by Mao's revolutionary ideology; frequent visits to rural China for learning from the peasants and the People's Liberation Army (PLA), combined with significant doses of Marxism and Leninism, were then the pillars of the education pattern. It was only towards the last part of his studies at the university in 1977, after the deaths of Mao and Zhou in 1976, that examinations were re-introduced in university courses, which he cleared for his graduation.

On valediction from the Tsinghua University in 1979, Xi Jinping worked for three years as secretary to Geng Biao, the then vice-premier and minister of national defence in the Chinese government. In 1982, designing his upward travel within the Party, he chose to leave the post and Beijing, to work as a deputy secretary in the northern province of Hebei; three years later, he moved on as vice-mayor of Xiamen in Fujian province. It was during this tenure that Xi married Peng Liyuan in 1987, a singer of repute and also holding high positions in the CCP because of her singing talent.[3]

From 1999 to 2008, Xi Jinping gained substantially in his standing in the CCP, holding deputy secretarial and gubernatorial positions in various provinces, overlooking environmental conservation, restructuring provincial industrial infrastructure, and also overseeing the preparations for the summer Olympic Games in Beijing; the Games got international recognition for China, and also elevated his standing in the Party. Xi, slowly and steadily, further consolidated his position in the Party, when in 2007, he was also selected as one of the nine members of the Standing Committee (reduced to seven, in 2012) of the CCP's Politburo, a promotion that indicated his inclusion in the shortlist of likely successors to Hu Jintao.

Xi's status in the CCP was further reinforced with his election as vice-president of China in 2008; he used this position to concentrate on environmental conservation and developing relations with other nations to gain experience in a broad spectrum, as a possible step towards gaining the ultimate position! In October 2010, there was another indicator of Xi Jinping moving to the apex position, when he was appointed as the deputy chairman of the Central Military Commission (CMC), a post generally considered as a stepping-stone to the presidency and the chairmanship of the CMC. In November 2012, Xi Jinping was formally elected as the general secretary of the CCP, and also appointed as the chairman of the CMC, the post which Hu Jintao vacated. Xi Jinping was voted as the president of China by the National People's Congress on March 14, 2013.

Xi Jinping Establishes Himself

Xi Jinping, as said above, was quite unknown to the world at large, and also to many Chinese people, despite his 30 years of public service. On his election, however, he did not keep anyone guessing for long about his intentions of how he was going to run the country. On his appointment as the general secretary, Xi Jinping underscored his main concerns at a briefing to the media, the foremost being to fight the widespread corruption in the Party and its key pillars—the military (People's Liberation Army—PLA), the State-Owned Enterprises (SOEs), the internal security apparatus, as well as the principal propaganda machine (the print and social media)—and to ensure that the Party cadres do not forget their primary task of serving the people. The main theme of his address, however, was restoring China to its rightful position of primacy in the world order—a revival or rejuvenation of the Chinese nation. Towards this end, he often referred to China's long years of history, of how his predecessors, without really naming anyone, had attempted at a revival of the country and how the attempts had "failed one time after another".[4]

Even though quite a few diplomatic and economic achievements marked the pre-Xi period, some notable blemishes too, had surfaced in the political and economic arenas in China. The CCP had meandered from its ideology, and many of its 80 million members were now using it only as a means for personal gains, both monetary (corruption!) and political. While the era before Xi assumed power had seen a phenomenal growth of the Chinese economy, with major benefits for the people, the spread of welfare benefits, critically of healthcare, had not kept pace. Initiatives to change China's course, hence, were at the forefront of Xi Jinping's plans for reforms, all through as he rose through the Party ranks, and a nation-wide campaign was started on his assuming power.

A brief digression is needed here to explain China's organisational structure. Since its formation in 1921 with the assistance of the Soviet Union, the CCP, has expanded and established itself over the years. After the civil war and the formation of the People's Republic of China, the CCP has ruled the country and is today, considered to be one of the most stable single-party systems in the world. After 1949, some features were institutionalised to aid governance. These structured features defined the character of the CCP in the decades to follow, with the Organisation Department being the first to be put in place by Mao. This department, in its main role, dispenses favours to members for their loyalty, in the form of important positions, both within the government and Party, giving rise to factions or coteries. Political patronage and resolution of behind-the-scenes political battles to win key positions, comprise the central thought of Chinese politics as practised by the CCP. Decisions are arrived at through a web of hierarchical central Party positions, beginning at the helm with the general secretary, who is also the president of the country, and going down the many formalised institutions, through the PSC, to the Party

Congress—with a membership of more than 2,000—the Chinese People's Political Consultative Conference (CPPCC), and the CMC; other smaller, yet important institutions include the Secretariat to the Politburo and the PSC, and various other such-sized groups in the Central Committee, with a similar system in place in the judicial arena.[5]

Xi Jinping commenced his tenure as general secretary and president with a distinctive strategy and as a man in a hurry, as if not having much time at his disposal. On the domestic front, Xi and his team moved away from the collective leadership by assuming control of committees and commissions—directly or indirectly through protégés. In global affairs, forceful utterances and actions that had emerged during the later stages of Hu Jintao's tenure, were translated into a more assertive behaviour through some massive, and open land-reclamation and subsequent militarisation of the islands in the South China Sea (SCS). A combination with an aggressive economic diplomacy through the promotion of the 'One Belt One Road' (OBOR), later popularly known as the 'Belt and Road Initiative' (BRI), initiated purportedly for infrastructure and development projects in South and Southeast Asian, Central Asian, African and some EU countries, has given China more than a strategic toe-hold in those nations. Alongside, during the spread of the Covid pandemic in 2020, China has developed a cadre of confrontational diplomats, their style of diplomacy being dubbed as "wolf-warrior diplomacy", who have threatened and insulted politicians and elected representatives in possibly every continent.[6] All actions, however, both within and outside China, have been started, and the momentum maintained, dominantly focussing on China's rejuvenation and the achievement of Xi Jinping 'Chinese Dream'.

During the earlier part of his tenure, since 2012, Xi Jinping strengthened his authority rapidly within the Party. Control of all the most important leading committees and commissions is in his hands; the anti-corruption campaign has eliminated his political rivals and facilitated the rise of his own faction; mass campaigns, a euphemism for censorship, in the physical and social media, with some drastic internet regulations, have suppressed dissent and debate within the country. In the economic arena, the Xi Jinping-led China did earn international acclaim for some bold reforms that it unveiled during the third plenum of the 18th Party Congress in November 2013. Next to the anti-corruption campaign, doubling income levels has been another important facet of Xi's Chinese dream. Between Xi and his Prime Minister, Li Keqiang, their inheritance of a galloping economy has been given a boost, and China has continued as the second-largest economy in the world with an aim of beating USA to claim the top position, whilst continuing its hold over other economies as the world's largest exporter.

Shoring up his supremacy to ensure his unhindered continuation in office to realise his goals has been achieved through some deft political manoeuvring. Institutions involved in all spheres of governance have been modified; as aforementioned, the principle of joint leadership has been weakened by the taking over of political institutions, large and small, either by Xi himself or through his coterie. This has resulted in the dilution of the principle of rule by consensus or collective leadership—a practice introduced by Deng, and followed all through the years thereafter—rather than authoritarianism under a single ruler, as was practised by Mao. This has made Xi, already the pre-eminent leader of the CCP, the most powerful leader since Mao Zedong.

The single-man leadership of Mao was characterised by excesses, for which reason Deng had advocated the idea of collective leadership: taking decisions by a group of leaders. It was also visualised that such a methodology would permit power-sharing by different factions in the various committees and organisations. To articulate his thoughts to promote collective leadership, Deng had issued a series of documents, the primary being "Several Principles on the Political Life in the Party".[7]

Xi's moves to strengthen the CCP—to get it further involved in the running of the state and the civil society, to reinforce his position within the party cadre—include the attack on the Communist Youth League (CYL). The CYL, essentially the youth wing of the CCP, had for long been the source for inducting new blood and fresh ideas into the Party, but lacked any political power; it was only with Hu Jintao and Li Keqiang, erstwhile members of the CYL, reaching top positions of power in the Party, that the CYL finally got the recognition that it had been long seeking. It was, however, also perceived by Xi as the breeding ground for his political competitors, and, hence, his efforts to cut it down to size. In 2016, after a two-month audit by the Central Commission for Discipline Inspection

(CCDI) criticised it for its "aristocratic tendencies", the budget was reduced to half, and an undergraduate division of the CYL was closed.[8]

Xi Jinping's Vision and Reforms

The central theme of the vision that Xi Jinping elucidated on his taking over in October 2012 can be defined as the great rejuvenation of China—*zhonghua minzu weida fuxing*.[9] Amongst the key pillars of the Party that Xi Jinping had earmarked for reforms was the PLA, with an aim to rid it of corruption and transform it into a more modern, capable, and disciplined military. Xi Jinping wanted a strong and modern military for China, which would fight a 21st century war and prevail over adversaries to safeguard the country's economic development, territorial integrity, and also the survival of the CCP. Expounding the requirement for a sturdier and resilient military, Xi often reflected upon the period between the decay in the dynasties in the late 19th century, and the Japanese occupation in the 1930s and 1940s. In Xi's words, a "nation's backwardness in military affairs has a profound influence on a nation's security. I often peruse the annals of modern Chinese history and feel heartbroken at the tragic scenes of us being beaten because of our ineptitude."[10] Xi Jinping often also alluded to the insufficient efforts of his predecessors in rejuvenating the country and did not wish to repeat the same mistakes.

Xi Jinping had wanted to give new contours to the PLA since his early days of taking over the mantle of leadership, which included the chairmanship of the CMC. At the third plenum of the 18th Party Congress, in October 2013, Xi announced his intention of bringing about changes in the PLA, through an overhaul of the command structure, training and logistics systems, pruning the Services, introduction of fresh instructions and protocols governing military personnel, and strengthening cooperation between the civil and military departments of the government. Xi's assuming leadership of the group for the transformation also indicated his central role in the entire process; the masterplan was unveiled on New Year's Day 2016, and the plan has been implemented since then.

A second set of reforms was introduced at the 19th Party Congress wherein the CMC was trimmed from the earlier 11 members to seven; the Congress session also gave powers to Xi Jinping to handpick the members. This was a move probably manoeuvred by Xi himself to place people who he could trust and who would implement the remainder of his reforms' agenda; those either infirm, untrustworthy, or found too dishonest to serve, and all those who had been placed by his predecessors, were removed!

Xi Jinping's execution of his plan to reinforce his hold over the Party and the country can be summarised thus: First, his anti-corruption drive has got rid of some well-known names from amongst the members of the Politburo, the PSC and the CMC; this broad-based attack on his perceived competitors, from all walks of power, sends out a strong signal. Second, he has used his growth-in-the-Party years—from his exile in 1969 to about 1980, when he finished his graduation—to good use to display himself as a representative of the hinterland. This populist identity, coupled with the launch of his poverty alleviation programme, has severely limited the role and popularity of the CYL. Lastly, Xi's attack on elite politicians and their factions in the many institutions—at the central and provincial positions— and their replacement with his own protégés, has eclipsed any opposition that may have existed earlier; Xi has elevated his family and the friends he made during his days working on farms during the Cultural Revolution, or during his days at Tsinghua University, or when he had held provincial appointments. Thus, at the end of Xi's first tenure, during the 19th Party Congress, the numbers of dissenters in the Politburo, PSC, and the Central Committee, and even in the provinces, reduced drastically, giving Xi total control over Chinese politics through hand-picked appointments at all levels.[11]

It was with such support from his loyalists, firmly entrenched at all strata of the CCP, that Xi Jinping, today, appears poised to continue ruling the country indefinitely. During the Mao era, there were no term limits for the presidency, however, between 1982 and 2017, the Chinese Constitution stipulated a fixed tenure of not more than two consecutive terms of five years each. In 2018, during the National People's Congress, the Constitution was amended to abolish presidential term limits, by 2,958 in favour, two opposing and three abstaining votes.[12] The abolishment of the tenure aligned Xi's tenure in other appointments that he holds as the general secretary of the CCP, and chairman of the CMC, neither of which have a stipulated occupancy. With rivals having been sidelined through the anti-corruption purges, and Xi Jinping's decision to not nominate a successor, his intentions are clearly indicative of continuation beyond 2022, the year that he would have otherwise relinquished his post of general secretary during the 20th National Congress in October 2022!

Xi Jinping's Tenure Thus Far and Beyond

What China is today has been described by the dean of Peking University's School of International Relations, Jia Qingguo, as now "in the third thirty years of contemporary Chinese history", which many also call the "Third Revolution![13] What Mao Zedong once said in 1927, at the beginning of the Chinese civil war, "political power grows out of the barrel of the gun", Xi Jinping has followed to the letter.

Initially though, there was not much difference in Xi's call to fight corruption from that of his predecessors'; all had emphasised, at one time or the other, after accessing the post of general secretary, the dangers being posed to the very existence of the CCP by the rampant corruption within, and the immediate and restorative steps needed to weed it out. Yet, Xi's call for fighting corruption was different. From 2008 to 2012, he had led the campaign against corruption from within the top leadership as an effort to reinvigorate the Party. There, however, was a difference; from the very beginning of his tenure: in a continuation of the campaign of the preceding years, his efforts were more personal, profound, and more political than any of his predecessors, since Mao.

Over the years, wide-ranging regulations have been put in place to curb even the smallest of opportunities that may tempt officials, high and low, to misuse their power; protocols restrict the number of cars that an official may own, the size of their homes, and even whether they are permitted secretaries or not! The Chinese bureaucracy and the heads of economic institutions—private and State-Owned Enterprises (SOEs)—have also been included in the gambit of the anti-corruption efforts; senior officials—some close to erstwhile general secretaries—senior executives, and even ministers, in important ministries such as energy, railways, media, and resources, have either been formally arrested, prosecuted, and jailed, or just simply detained and disappeared.[14] The anti-corruption campaign has not waned since

Xi Jinping assumed power in 2012, rather, Xi has re-emphasised his commitment towards continuing the fight against corruption. He displayed his resolve in a speech delivered during the 19th Party Congress, "The people resent corruption most; and corruption is the greatest threat our Party faces," further mentioning that he would now take the fight to the "people's doorsteps", through the introduction of a new system for the discipline inspection of local Party committees.[15]

A major manifestation of Xi's consolidation of power, and endorsed by the 19th Party Congress in October 2017, and the 13th National People's Congress in 2018, is the formal inclusion of "Xi Jinping Thought on Socialism with Chinese Characteristics for a New Era" as part of the Chinese Constitution. The earlier leaders, Deng, Jiang and Hu, were granted such recognition only after they had formally exited politics; in the current leadership, with Xi Jinping, it has been done at the near commencement of what appears to be a long march in his political career! What is more remarkable is that this is the first time that a living leader's ideology and beliefs have been written into the Party's Constitution, after the enshrining of Mao's Thoughts. Having 'officially' abolished the tenure, a further indicator of Xi Jinping's unparalleled political power appeared with Xi chairing six high-level groups, as well as almost all of the major policy-making central committees and commissions. With this, he has assumed total power to get his loyalists placed in the seven-man Standing Committee of the Politburo, the 20-person wider Politburo, and the 209-member Central Committee, thus, smoothening the wrinkles in his political journey much more than from what it was when he started after the 18th Party Congress in October 2012.

The widespread anti-corruption campaign with the associated purging of Xi Jinping's opponents, and, hence, leading to an extraordinary consolidation of power to himself, the decision to alter the term-limits, has, as could be expected, led to a growth of a political backlash, causing concern to Xi and his supporters. Although the dissent is in small and silent pockets thus far, it has produced groups of highly discontented officials; retired leaders whose power has diminished, officials and business people frustrated with curbs on their spending, judicial officials and political activists concerned with the opaqueness of the reforms, are central against Xi Jinping's moves.[16]

While detractors initiated closed-door debates, censorship was immediately applied to any discussions that appeared on the Chinese social media. State-controlled media such as the *People's Daily*, have been conducting 'fire-fighting' campaigns through well-timed insertions in the dailies, taking pains to explain the reforms, especially the extension of the presidential tenure, which it said, does not necessarily mean "leadership for life".[17] Within the Party too, there are groups of dissent that may be termed as the "silent minority",[18] which, however, cannot be expected to create any resistance to Xi Jinping's push towards reforms and consolidation. Nonetheless, with an almost absolute centralisation of power and decision-making by a single individual, Chinese officials are concerned about the adverse effects on political efficacy and economic growth; additionally, such a campaign has made Xi himself susceptible to any single, large-scale adverse contingency that may arise in the future, be it in the SCS, Korean peninsula, Taiwan, Hong Kong, or any major social disruption within the country. Such a case occurred in January 2020, when the health authorities, overseen by the Party delayed action on the outbreak of the SARS-COVID-19 virus, presumably due to Xi's non-availability to give a decision!

What Xi Jinping has sought to achieve by the reforms introduced in the PLA between 2015 and 2018 is the making of a modern war-fighting machine, not only with new weapon platforms and cutting-edge technology, but also with a matching contemporary organisational set-up, which included personnel changes in key positions. Apart from this, was also his desire to revitalise the Party control over the PLA, members of which had tended to drift away from the Party ideology, had become aloof from the people, and had prioritised their own interests over those of the Party. The reforms, of course, also had an ulterior aim of elevating Xi's status and authority within all arms of the PLA, and, hence, within the Party itself, which was essential for his anti-corruption campaign.

Some of Xi's efforts have inherent contradictions, such as the negative impact of the anti-corruption campaign, discontinuation of market reforms, increasing control of the state on the economy and massive spending on defence. These policies, at variance with those of Xi's predecessors, are not liked by many[19], and have had an adverse effect on the overall economic growth. The 19th Party Congress has laid out the plan of what Deng

Xiaoping had once described as the third phase of China's modern economic development; a phase, in which, China would seek to attain parity in income levels with the Organisation for Economic Cooperation and Development (OECD) average.[20] The unmatched increased mandate to deliver, created by removing the term limits on China's presidency, has given the country's economy and society a complicated transition, wherein success could see China become the largest economy in the world, and failure could leave the country in turmoil. Analysts, both outside and within China, believe that it can be done; with hardly any impediments—the only question is how the transition would be managed, both economically and politically, more so during the trying times of the pandemic.

Ever since Xi assumed power, China has relatively closed its doors, rather than opening them. Foreign investment and the corporate working environment have been adversely affected with the suppression of civil society and foreign Non-Governmental Organisations (NGOs), not just due to Xi's anti-corruption campaign, but with the xenophobic apprehensions of the current youth being adversely influenced by the supposedly demented Western culture. In April 2013, the CCP circulated the *Communique on the Current State of the Ideological Sphere*, later referred to as Document 9, going by the sequential order of the communiques issued that year![21] The document detailed the profound clash between the liberal Western ideas that were presumed to have permeated the Chinese society and the ideology of the CCP. The Party leadership was urged to guard against the seven political threats, which included, amongst others, constitutionalism, civil society, negative opinions and interpretations of the past times, general standards, and the endorsement of the Western idea of freedom to the media. It called on all Party members to resist infiltration of external thoughts, renew their commitment to work "in the ideological sphere," and remain vigilant against all ideas, institutions, and people that appeared to be a threat to the single Party rule.[22]

At the release of Document 9, some observers felt that the Document was the opinion of a small cross-section consisting mainly of conservatives. When the harsh clampdown started against human rights activists and lawyers, media, academia, and other such independent thinkers, and then became a norm, the viewpoints, however, changed. The writing was on the wall that it was the central leadership, with Xi at the forefront, that was guiding the CCP cadre. The first to be targeted were the universities, followed by the Chinese Academy of Social Sciences (CASS), starting in 2013 itself and carrying on through to 2017. In 2013, Xi had proclaimed that "politicians should run the newspapers"; continuing his tirade against the media, in his efforts to bring it to heel, he then said the media "must be surnamed Party" (*bixu xing dang*).[23] The control of the media was not restricted to just articles and programmes on sensitive political issues; in March 2016, a new set of rules stipulated that shows depicting a 'luxurious lifestyle', or 'the dark side of society', and 40 other such topics, could not be shown either on TV or social media; this was a marked increase from an earlier similar set of rules issued in 2010![24]

A predominant step that was taken by the Chinese government in its efforts to curb the infiltration of foreign ideas and values that did not conform to its ideology, was the enactment of a law in January 2017 named Law on the Management of Foreign Non-Governmental Organisations. Surprisingly though, the law was passed after wide-ranging deliberations and debate between the Chinese government and non-government agencies, and their opposite numbers from foreign countries. As per the new law, all NGOs have to be registered and affiliated with a government agency to ensure oversight on their activities and personnel within the country, including the raising of funds.

Why did Xi Jinping, right from the time of taking over the reins in 2013, and the CCP, take the 'bull by the horns' to restrict the adoption of foreign ideas and values, with strong determination, even vengeance? This was necessitated because of the findings of an old survey conducted in the Ningxia Party School, in 2002, which had shown some very adverse results: among the urban residents of Ningxia, "25 per cent did not believe in the cause of socialist construction, 50 per cent doubted the CCP's role as vanguard of the working class, 65 per cent felt that they were no longer the 'masters in their own house' (*guojia de zhuren*), and 79 per cent had lost their emotional ties to the Party."[25] Xi Jinping has given legitimacy to both Mao's and Deng Xiaoping's reforms, stating that each supports the other, and also validated Confucius' ideas and beliefs, to revive these amongst the people and convince them that the CCP and the political system are oriented towards meeting their needs. Xi has also sought to reinforce the belief in the people that it is the value system of the CCP and its right to lead that would eventually enable China to occupy its destined position in the global order as the sole superpower!

Dissent has been present in the every day dealings of Xi's tenure, suppressed, at times, by the anti-corruption campaign, or by threats and coercions, or by imposing censorship over publications and media—print, visual, and social. Despite all the means available to the CCP and the government, dissenting voices continue to make themselves heard, since not all are convinced about the route Xi Jinping is taking the country on. There are calls for increased political openness, free media, and freedom of speech, as the activists feel that that is the correct way to address social ills. While most of Xi Jinping's critics attack his policies, there are some who make personal attacks too. Although the debates and discussions take place behind closed doors, activists continue to feel the heat!

The first five-year tenure has seen major progress in transformation of governance structures. Some very visible changes that have taken place are as follows:

- The principle of collective leadership is, all but, non-existent.
- Political power has been centralised as never seen after Mao.
- The role of the Party has become quite evident in civil society, the educational system, and not to forget, the media.
- The influence of foreign NGOs has been limited through the new registration process.

Nevertheless, the reforms and 'strengthening' of the CCP have also had some contradicting results, such as the effect of the anti-corruption campaign on the economic growth due to delays in decision-making because of the centralisation of power. With the passage of time, more adverse effects could emerge, but it is unlikely that these would be shared with the public or the world due to China's inherent secretive nature. Other causes for China's shrinking economy include the international sanctions on China due to its alleged role in the spread of the COVID-19 virus and the ensuing global pandemic.

Despite the flattering official media reports, and the many massive and grand parades displaying new armament and weapons, the PLA too, has not been free of dissent. Murmurs of dissent are not just against the anti-corruption and anti-cronyism campaigns within the PLA, but on the professional front too. While individuals and smaller fighting groups—platoons, companies—may be able to demonstrate their fighting prowess, the establishment of joint theatre commands has its related issues of being able to deliver in the battlefield, and not the least being the army losing the predominant position that it had enjoyed for many decades, to the other two services. Some veteran officers, reportedly, had expressed reservations during a protest in front of the Ba Yi building on October 11, 2017, on the propounded efficacy of the PLA after the geographical reorganisation, the resultant reshuffle of key posts, the liaison between the civil agencies and the military to share intelligence, and other related issues, leading analysts to question Xi's objectives in the PLA reforms.[26]

Xi Jinping's dream to see China setting a new world order has also been shattered to quite an extent, with his pet project of the BRI showing signs of getting derailed even before the outbreak of the pandemic of 2020, and now, since the outbreak, there are little or no hopes of it getting back on track. There are reports that the lending under the BRI has drastically reduced from $ 75 billion in 2016 to just $3 billion in 2020.[27] Notwithstanding the impeded growth of the economy, China, or it can be said, Xi Jinping, claims to have achieved a "human miracle of eliminating extreme poverty" and lifting millions above the poverty line of $2.30 in daily income, in a short period between 2015, when he vowed to eradicate poverty, and 2020, and, thus, build a "moderately prosperous society" by the 100th anniversary of the Party.[28] While the standard of living of an average Chinese has improved, these claims have been received with doubts by the Western analysts and China watchers.

End Musings

The studied silence on the declaration of Xi's successor, and the earlier announcement of the abolition of the limitation on the tenure for the president are ample indications that Xi Jinping is going to be around after the 20th Party Congress in 2022. The 19th Congress has accepted the new rules and spelt out important and appropriate principles for international engagement—political and economic—but the path to be followed appears hazy today due to various reasons, not the least being the outbreak of the Covid pandemic since March 2020.

Xi Jinping is at the peak of his power graph, notwithstanding the local and global spread of the Covid virus; if official statistics are to be believed, China has been the most successful country in tackling the pandemic with strict lockdowns and the commencement of its vaccination programme for its citizens, much before the Western nations, especially USA, which is considered to be its main competitor in all spheres. During the difficult times of the Covid pandemic, again, if the official statistics are to be believed, China's economy has been the best performing globally. It is, therefore, no small surprise, that some analysts are saying that contemporary China has had no leader since Mao, with such absolute power, leading it to a prosperous future.

Wanting to rename the 21st century as the century of China's rise, instead of what was being called the Asian century, China has apparently had no qualms in threatening global security to achieve this objective. With the creation of the image of an infallible leader, and contradictions appearing in the reforms, Xi Jinping may now find it very difficult to re-establish himself as the great, paramount leader, both within China and globally. Although he did achieve some successes in developing the Chinese economy and international relations, today, however, after the outbreak of the Covid-pandemic, the Chinese image has taken a beating. Within the country, there are many political and military leaders, who have lost their positions and privileges due to the anti-corruption campaign, waiting on the sidelines, for Xi to trip and fall! Cai Xia, a political scientist, and once a loyal member of the CCP, was expelled in August 2020 for a critical interview to *The Guardian* in June 2020, in which she had revealed widespread opposition amongst the cadres of the CCP to the policies of Xi Jinping; she has emphatically stated in her interview that Xi Jinping has singlehandedly "killed a party and a country".[29] The voices of dissent seem to have been growing louder, but simultaneously, the voices have been silenced.

Will Xi Jinping really trip and fall? It is anybody's guess!

Notes

1. Elizabeth C. Economy, *The Third Revolution* (Oxford University Press, South Asia edition, 2018).

2. Melissa Albert, "Xi Jinping : President of China", Britannica, https://www. britannica.com/biography/Xi-Jinping, accessed on January 16, 2021.

3. Ibid.

4. "Full Text of Xi's Address to the Media", *China Daily*, November 16, 2012, http:// www.chinadaily.com.cn/china/2012cpc/2012-11/16/content_15934514.htm, accessed on September 10, 2020.

5. Richard McGregor, *The Party: The Secret World of China's Communist Rulers* (Harper Collins, June 2, 2010), as quoted in Srijan Shukla, "The Rise of the Xi Gang", *Firstpost*, February 15, 2021, https://www.firstpost.com/world/the-rise-of-the-xi-gang-a-closer-look-at-factional-politics-in-the-chinese-communist-party-9304181.html, accessed on March 1, 2021.

6. Air Mshl Dhiraj Kukreja, "China's Wolf-Warrior Diplomacy", *Defence and Security Alert*, Web Edition, June 9, 2020, https://www.dsalert.org/chinas-wolf-warrior-diplomacy.

7. Srijan Shukla, "The Rise of the Xi Gang", *Firstpost*, February 15, 2021, www. firstpost.com, accessed on March 1, 2021.

8. Economy, n. 1.

9. n. 4.

10. Phillip C. Saunders, Arthur S. Ding, Andrew Scobell, Andrew N.D. Yang, and Joel Wuthnow, eds, *Chairman Xi Remakes the PLA* (Washington DC, NDU Press, 2019).

11. Shukla, n. 7.

12. James Doubek, "China Removes Presidential Term Limits, Enabling Xi Jinping To Rule Indefinitely" March 11, 2018, Nevada Public Radio (knpr.org), accessed on March 1, 2021.

13. Ibid.

14. Economy, n. 1.

15. Xi Jinping in a speech delivered at the 19th National Congress of the Communist Party of China, October 18, 2017, "Secure a Decisive Victory in Building a Moderately Prosperous" (china.org.cn), accessed on March 3, 2021.

16. Economy, n. 1.

17. Kevin Rudd, "Understanding China's Rise Under Xi Jinping", in a speech delivered to cadets at the US Military Academy, West Point, on March 5, 2018. Transcript

available on https://asiasociety.org/policy-institute/understanding-chinas-rise-under-xi-jinping, accessed on January 10, 2021.

18. Economy, n. 1.

19. Ibid.

20. "Xi's New Power and China's Economic and Social Goals", East Asia Forum, accessed on January 10, 2021.

21. Economy, n. 1.

22. "Document 9: A ChinaFile Translation", ChinaFile, November 8, 2013, accessed on March 5, 2021.

23. Suisheng Zhao, "Xi Jinping's Maoist Revival", *Journal of Democracy*, July 2016, Vol 27, Number 3, Zhao-27-3.pdf (journalofdemocracy.org), accessed on March 5, 2021.

24. Josh Horwitz and Zheping Huang, "China's New Television Rules Ban Homosexuality, Drinking, and Vengeance", March 3, 2016, *Quartz* (qz.com), accessed on March 5, 2021.

25. Heike Holbig, "Remaking the CCP's Ideology", *Journal of Current Chinese Affairs*, Vol 38, No 3, 2009 (uni-hamburg.de), accessed on March 10, 2021.

26. Saunders et al., n. 10.

27. "Xi Jinping's Dream Project 'Belt and Road Initiative' in Trouble Amid China's Shrinking Economy", *The Mint ePaper*, March 14, 2021 (livemint.com), accessed on March 14, 2021.

28. "Xi Jinping Declares China Created 'Human Miracle' of Eliminating Extreme Poverty", NDTV, February 25, 2021 (ndtv.com), accessed on February 25, 2021.

29. "Xi Jinping Expels Party Members as Dissent Grows in Chinese Communist Party", WION, August 18, 2020, https://www.wionews.com/world/xi-jinping-expels-party-members-as-dissent-grows-in-chinese-communist-party-321547, accessed on March 15, 2021.

6.   Is China Making a New World Order

Opening Thoughts

In June 1945, in San Francisco, 50 countries signed the charter that created the United Nations Organisation (UNO aka UN); the pact had a vacant seat for Poland, for it to join a few months later as the 51st founding member. Compared to its predecessor, the League of Nations, the UN has exceeded expectations in some ways; principally, that unlike the League of Nations, which was set up after World War I, it has survived all these years, with the addition of as many as 193 nations as members, thanks largely to decolonisation, and notwithstanding the many conflicts that the world continues to see, there has been no third world war!

The UN developed as a fairly successful organisation and was instrumental in stopping wars that broke out in the initial days of its inception and also initiating social growth in underdeveloped nations. Notwithstanding its successes, some important weaknesses have come to the forefront in the recent past. A ready example that comes to mind is the global challenge of terrorism, which continues unabated; far from the UN Security Council (UNSC) being able to control the incidents, it has failed to even arrive at a consensus for a definition of terrorism! Similarly, other organisations and treaties, such as the World Trade Organisation (WTO) and the Nuclear Non-Proliferation Treaty (NPT), which have the UN at their apex, have been plagued by in-house issues, the global attempts to tackle the 'peaceful' rise of China, and, importantly by the disregard, and the antagonistic attitude of the country that was its chief architect and sponsor, the United States of America. Nonetheless, the global order is worth saving. As Dag Hammarskjold, a celebrated secretary-general, said, "The UN was not created to take mankind to heaven, but to save humanity from hell."[1]

The Origin of the Expression: 'World Order'

US President Woodrow Wilson, used the term, "World Order", in his Fourteen Points agenda for world peace, while calling for a League of Nations, after the devastation caused by World War I;[2] this was one of the first and probably the most well-known Western uses of the term. After the Treaty of Versailles that brought an end to the war, it was felt that peaceful coexistence in the world would not be possible as before, and that the fighting had been a conduit to the deteriorating international politics. Since the entry of America was instrumental in ending the war, it was given the privilege to make the world safer by spelling out a charter for a peace organisation. President Wilson insisted on the formation of a new world order, which would be unaffected by the prevailing power politics, with an emphasis on collective security, democracy and self-governance. Paradoxically, while President Wilson had faith in the League of Nations to instil cooperation among nations, the US Senate refused approval for becoming its member![3]

The League of Nations failed in its prime charter of managing international politics and providing collective security, leading to the phrase, 'new world order', being sparingly used when plans were being made for the formation of the UN after World War II. However, the term was used extensively when discussing the creation of new multinational organisations, such as the US-Europe security coalition of the North Atlantic Treaty Organisation (NATO), International Monetary Fund (IMF), and International Bank for Reconstruction and Development.

All through the 20th century, although there was no third world war, the two major superpowers, USA and USSR (now divided into independent nations), were engaged in a Cold War that, at times, brought the two nations on the brink of a major conflict, either directly or through their proxies. Skirmishes and localised wars were contained and the UN, while continuously expanding its strength, held together the comity of nations: the world order held fast! It was only after the collapse of USSR in 1991 and the end of the Cold War that USA became the *de facto* world leader and its utterances and actions in international politics set the tone for diplomatic, economic, and political dialogues and propositions, at times, much to the annoyance of other nations.

The phrase 'new world order', in recent times, was widely discussed and used from the end of the Cold War, but it remained undefined. Presidents Mikhail Gorbachev of the erstwhile USSR and George HW Bush of USA made an attempt to outline the post-Cold War period with the use of the term, hoping that the 'spirit of great power cooperation' might come about with its use. President Gorbachev's initial articulation was wide-ranging and unworkable, and, hence, he could not further it, being constrained by the arising crises due to the crumbling Soviet system. President Bush's vision was not less restricted: "A hundred generations have searched for this elusive path to peace, while a thousand wars raged across the span of human endeavour. Today, that new world is struggling to be born, a world quite different from the one we've known."[4] However, given the new status of USA as being the sole power, Bush's vision was plausible: "... there is no substitute for American leadership."[5]

The US leadership was primarily applicable to its allies, European and a few others, which were bound to it through traditional treaties and other agreements, related mainly to security and the economy. For such a regulating authority accorded to a nation, to be acceptable to the world, its actions have to be planned with a great deal of accountability and, more importantly, with the inescapable need of the nation to be ethical in all it does, always! As is applicable for leadership at any level in any organisation, the proverbial 'moral high-ground' is the only position that a world leader can operate from, with any authority.

While the phrase 'new world order', as used to usher in the post-Cold War era in the early 1990s, may not have been well defined, it did appear to have three distinct periods. The usage was first by the Soviets, and later by USA, prior to the Malta Conference, and thereafter during President Bush's speech of September 11, 1990. Initially, the two presidents discussed the new world order to deal with nuclear disarmament and security arrangements in the immediate aftermath at the end of the Cold War. The scope of the term was then opened out to be inclusive of actions to bolster the UNO, and great power cooperation on a range of economic and security issues, which concerned NATO, the Warsaw Pact, and European integration. These various expectations were deliberated upon in great detail during the Malta Conference, held on December 2-3, 1989, which then included German reunification, human rights, and the polarity of the international system. President Bush, however, stole the initiative from President Gorbachev during the build-up to the Gulf War, 'Desert Storm' in 1991; the 'new world order' was now to focus on international cooperation and regional crises with a UN concurrence, as a clearance to act against Iraq. The *Washington Post*, in an editorial emphasised this occurrence: "This superpower cooperation demonstrates that the Soviet Union has joined the international community, and that in the new world order, Saddam faces not just the US but the international community itself."[6] The US leadership over a multinational coalition, with a capacity to wield overwhelming military power, demonstrated American primacy in a distinctively unipolar post-Cold War world, announcing a new world order!

New World Order in the 21st Century

Henry Kissinger, the veteran diplomat, while participating in a World Affairs Council Press Conference at the Regent Beverly Wilshire Hotel in Los Angeles, on April 19, 1994, stated, "The New World Order cannot happen without US participation, as we are the most significant single component. Yes, there will be a New World Order, and it will force the United States to change its perceptions."[7]

Leading to the 21st century, various heads of states, mainly from the Western nations spoke about the 'new world order' in many forums, alluding to what Henry Kissinger had said. Just after the terrorist attacks in New York, in September 2001, commonly known as 9/11, former UK Prime Minister Tony Blair, during a speech on November 13, 2001, stated, "There is a new world order, like it or not"[8], in reference to the 9/11 attacks and the 'war on terror' thereafter to dissuade any such further actions. Analysts argued that the 9/11 terror attacks would not have any enduring geopolitical impact and that they were the effective end to the 20th century; how wrong they were! Michael Howard, the distinguished war historian at the University of Oxford, said that while the terrorist threat "will never entirely go away, I suspect that once we have hunted down the present lot of conspirators the world will return to business as usual."[9] There were others who projected significant changes, but very few believed that the US would be still fighting in West Asia almost two decades later; once again, how wrong they were!

On the other hand, the eccentric Iranian President Mahmoud Ahmedinejad, in an interview with the Islamic Republic of Iran Broadcasting (IRIB), called for disrupting the influence of the Western nations by forming a new world order. He noted that "it was time to propose new ideologies for running the world...based on world peace, global collective security, reciprocity and justice"; he went on to term the Western powers as "tyrannical regimes and arrogant powers, whose policies in countries like Iraq and Afghanistan were failing."[10] The interview, which came at the end of Israel's 23-day offensive against Gaza, was expectedly condemned, but not by all nations; surprisingly, it also caused disagreements within the political parties in Israel!

Apart from the momentous happenings related to the end of the Cold War in 1991 at the end of the last century, and similarly, the terrorist attacks of September 2001 in the beginning of the 21st century, the world has seen other major geopolitical shocks too, where analysts and leaders grossly miscalculated the long-term effects on their society, politics, governance, economy, trade and development. US policy-makers misjudged the financial crisis of 2007-09, when they opted to let the Lehman Brothers fail in September 2008; it was incorrectly conjectured that allowing the failure of the Lehman Brothers would not be the basis for the failure of other companies. Across the Atlantic, EU officials never thought that the euro zone would be susceptible to exposure, reasoning that the crisis had originated in USA; apprehensions that it would affect global financial markets were dismissed. The collaboration in responding to the crisis, among the G-20 countries, especially the US and China, made many a nation's leadership blind to the events leading to the forthcoming great power competition. With the oblivion, was the combination of rising nationalistic tendencies in many governments. As the historian Adam Tooze argued in 2012, the mainstream right-wing populism may have ebbed, but many more shocks—Brexit, the surprise win of Donald Trump in the US presidential elections, Russia's annexation of Crimea and China's escalating role in the world financial and political system—lay in the future.[11]

China, gradually, has become increasingly assertive in the first two decades of the 21st century, becoming pushy and aggressive in all spheres—economic, political and diplomatic—while meticulously building up its military capabilities. While China has kept its global ambitions formally undeclared by continuously emphasising on its 'peaceful rise', it has not hidden its aspirations to be the principal regional power in Asia and second to USA, or even standing abreast with it, on the global scene. Its actions in the South China Sea (SCS) are a display of this national objective. China's ambition has been underscored by its open confrontation with the US and its allies in the region that China considers its own backwaters, more so during the widespread outbreak of the COVID-19 pandemic from early 2020 onwards. The timing could not have been more providential for China and disastrous for USA and the world at large.

The threat to the rules-based global order seems to be weighing on everyone's mind, including USA, whose position as the sole superpower in the world is now threatened, not by its old Cold War rival, Russia, but an assertive and ambitious China of the 21st century. If the US pulls back, intentionally or otherwise, then other countries need to take the initiative to maintain the rules-based world order. For many years, countries had become habituated to seeing America take the lead; it is time now for the middling powers like Japan, France and Germany, and the rising ones like India and Indonesia, to take the initiative for the maintenance of the rules-based world order. Any dithering will risk the world moving towards the situation that existed in the 1920s and 1930s, and moving on to the 1940s and 1950s, that first forced the creation of the League of Nations and then the UN and other institutions.

To be sure, the world order was already undergoing a slow and steady transmutation. Globalisation norms had been threatened by the rise of social and political movements in many nations, for maintaining national identity; the rise of deep patriotic feelings, and even anger, due to a trust deficit and a general erosion of belief in multilateral agreements, are indicative of a departure from the established norms. The increased antipathy between USA and China—with other countries caught in a vice between the so-called American 'I-am-the-best complex' and China's pragmatic deviations from Marxist ideology—has further made the people more aware of this departure. It remains to be seen if the rapid spread of the pandemic will accelerate the conclusion of these processes or push the world to an entirely new path altogether. It is a certainty, however, that the COVID-19 pandemic would be a turning point in the history of the human race, just like the Great Depression, World War II and the 2008 financial crisis.

The UN is an amalgamation of exasperating and irksome bureaucracy, and, at times, hypocritical institutions: the Human Rights Council (UNHRC) reprimands Israel for its treatment meted out to the Palestinians, yet does not raise its voice against China's behaviour towards the Uighurs; the UNSC has appropriated veto powers to Britain and France, albeit much moderated since 1945, but adamantly refuses to induct new members like Japan, Germany, Brazil, India or any nation from the African continent. Yet the global world order is worth the attempt for saving.

The task of safeguarding the system from the forces of disorder, however, is easier said than done. One threat is the growing acrimony between America and China, which could bring the working of international institutions to a standstill. This has been intensified by competing parallel financial and security arrangements at a time when the world and its institutions are in the midst of a struggle to cope with the rise of China and preserve the existing and fragile world order that is purportedly under threat from it. Another is that America may continue its careless treatment of multilateral institutions; the authority of the World Health Organisation (WHO) was diluted at the peak of the pandemic by USA. Ever since President Trump's election in 2016, he walked out of many multilateral treaties and agreements; to name a few: the Iran Nuclear Deal, the Trans-Pacific Partnership, Paris Climate Agreement, which further led to the destabilisation of the world order and weakened the US leadership.

Thankfully, the world has not yet reached the point of no return. For decades, as aforementioned, the self-reliant, yet, second rung, powers, have looked up to USA for assistance and maintenance of the world order; today, they are obliged to involve themselves in global affairs a little more. France and Germany have created an alliance that is open to other countries; another proposal is for nine democracies to form a "committee to save the world order"[12]—these include Japan, Germany, Australia and Canada, which together generate a third of the world's GDP. There have been occasions when countries have got together to put USA in a bind; after a former Russian spy, now living in Britain was subjected to a chemical-poisoning attack, the imposition of sanctions on Russia by the Western nations forced USA to react and impose sanctions too. Although USA continues to be a leading power in the world, there are times, when the world must work without it, even if it may be not the best option! After President Trump walked away from the Trans-Pacific Partnership (TPP)—a mega trade deal between 12 Pacific Rim nations—the other members went ahead and planned deals amongst themselves. When hindered at the World Trade Organisation (WTO), countries are now resorting to forming regional and bilateral trade arrangements, such as one between Japan and the EU and another between 28 countries in Africa.

The prime requisite is to protect the international order. While, on the one hand, USA has reduced its financial contribution to the UN, China's stature is growing along with its contributions; bypassing Japan's contribution of 8.5 per cent, it now pays 12 per cent of the UN budget, as compared with one per cent in 2000; four of the UN's 15 specialised agencies are headed by Chinese diplomats, while America heads just one! If countries do not organise themselves, China's policies and views on national sovereignty and resistance to intervention will become predominant in the system, despite its blatant human rights violations. China's attempts to make the UN a tool for achieving its hegemonic ambitions could lead to a total disruption in the world order.

If China's influence in the world order is on the rise through its actions in the UN and amongst other countries through its Belt and Road Initiative (BRI) and promises of soft loans, the question then arises: is the US' influence waning? The international order, which had been in place since the end of World War II, had came under threat due to the disdainful and often irresponsible actions of President Trump. There is a thought though that America had been gradually losing its dominance in world affairs even before President Trump's confrontational and loud-mouthed foreign policy positions. The culmination of the Cold War signalled the beginning of a transfer of power among the nations of the world, which has been evolving further this century. It cannot be wished away by saying "American influence is waning," since America continues to be a dominant nation in all realms—economic, military, and in technology—but for some time now, American influence has definitely been wearing away. This became more evident due to the changes championing "America First" seclusion. President Trump's policies swung the political mood, with US involvement only in selected domains, limited to areas of vital interest to it; economic nationalism became the most important issue, leading to American friends and foes alike, paying close attention and planning their actions accordingly.

It is not just the countries of the world that are yet to come to grips with the change; even within USA, neither American political party has really understood what is happening! It is not only China and Russia that are a challenge to America's global functions; an increasing number of countries are playing an independent and dominant role in regional economic and security developments. Tensions between the West and Russia, and between the US and China, had been going well beyond competing interests in eastern Ukraine or over uninhabited rocks in the South China Sea. This situation, however, has changed rapidly since the beginning of 2020, when the news of the COVID-19 virus purportedly spreading out of China came to be known, and then the entire world got affected by the pandemic.

A pushy and aggressive China has risen now, with the confidence to exhibit a show of strength in the global economy, challenging the US, ignoring, to a certain extent, the trade wars initiated by President Trump. It has propagated its one-party example for economic growth as against the democratic model, reshaped atolls and placed its military on artificial islands in the South China Sea—ignoring world opinion and the judgement against it by the International Court of Justice (ICJ)—and gone on to create a military base in Djibouti. China has created new regional multilateral organisations for security discussions, such as the ASEAN+ and SCO; bilaterally, it is offering loans on purportedly easy terms through the BRI, in the garb of developing infrastructure in the economically weak nations of Asia, Africa and Latin America, thus, also spreading its political influence. Neither USA nor any of the other developed economies, have either been able to slow down the Chinese economic juggernaut or contain its growing power. China is changing the rules of the world order as per its liking, ignoring the likes or dislikes of the US or the world!

China in The New World Order

In the past three decades or thereabouts, the world has witnessed some historic events, which may even be termed earth-shaking, that have had a huge impact on the emergence of a new world order. The termination of Communism in Eastern Europe, the fall of the Berlin Wall with the unification of Germany, and the collapse of USSR marked the wind-up of the bipolar order and the end of the Cold War. NATO's intercession in the former Yugoslavia and expansion of NATO into Central and Eastern Europe—much to the annoyance of Russia—strengthened America's presence in Europe. The signing of the Maastricht Treaty, the establishment of the European Union (EU), a creation of a single European currency— euro—and three rounds of EU enlargement made the EU a big player in the international arena. Then, at the turn of the century, came the 9/11 terrorist attack, which started the War on Terror, getting America and its allies into a longstanding conflict in Afghanistan and Iraq. A global financial crisis in 2008 caused a worldwide economic downturn, with the EU debt crisis destabilising the European economy, and, at one time, even threatening the very continuance of the euro itself.

China, as the growing giant of Asia, had initiated its economic reforms and openness to international markets in 1978; over the years, the changes have yielded results. China has sustained a high economic growth rate in the world for many years, becoming one of the global economic driving forces. As per predictions, it surpassed Japan (see Fig. 6.1) to become the second largest economy in the world, next only to USA. Applying Confucian wisdom in its pragmatic foreign policy, it has succeeded in integrating itself into the global economic system.

Fig. 6.1: GDP (in trillions of dollars)

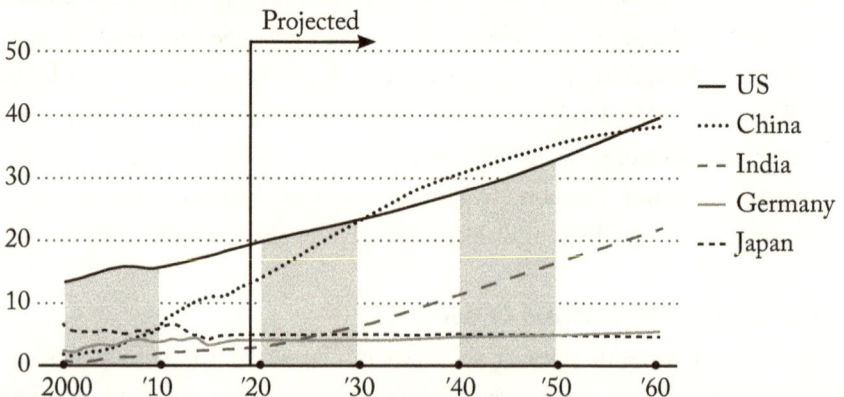

Source: Governments, Japan Centre for Economic Research (projections).

China's rise has powered its dream to be a major world power and a regional superpower and regain its rightful position in the comity of nations. Not only has its economy kept pace with its ambitions, President Xi Jinping has modified the political system in small steps ever since 2012, when he took over the reins as the general secretary of the Communist Party of China (CPC aka CCP), then as president in 2013, and taking the final step in 2018, of making himself the supreme leader by abolishing the restrictions on the number of tenures that a president can serve.

With major changes underway in the world, the new global order is evolving surely and steadily. There is general consensus that the world has been moving from unipolarity (USA) towards multipolarity; the new main players of international politics are the US, China, the EU and Russia. The impact that America once had may be on the wane now, but it still is the only major power with strong bonds in both Europe and Asia. It has a well-established market economy and is still the largest economy in the world. Combined with an effective financial system in place, the American dollar remains the largest international reserve currency. A strong military backs the economy, with China, however, fast closing the gap. There exists an assumption that the world has transformed into a multipolar world, but as Simon Tisdall opines, what has emerged is "a tripolar world, dominated by a weakening USA, a resurgent Russia, and an assertive China".[13]

With a revival of protectionism through President Trump's policies of 'America First' and the Brexit of 'Britain First', the Chinese president had called for a change in globalisation. At the 19th Party Congress, held between October 18-24, 2017, President Xi Jinping had called for a 'community of shared human destiny', elaborating China's vision: "We call on the people of all countries to work together to build a community with a shared future for mankind, to build an open, inclusive, clean, and beautiful world that enjoys lasting peace, universal security, and common prosperity"[14]. According to President Xi Jinping's suggestion, all nations, while pursuing own interests, should give due thought to the rightful concerns of other nations, thus, creating a mutually beneficial environment with a win-win global cooperation, as opposed to the existing concept of international relations—namely, one of disorder, power politics and a winner-takes-all dynamics. As per his idea, all human beings, having to share a common space of one earth, must learn to coexist. In China's thinking of a global society, economic liberalisation would continue in the world, while working towards a new system, more reasonable and all-encompassing, with shared human values.

President Xi Jinping, through this message, has pointed towards the part China would play in the evolving international order. The message, for those who would understand, was amply clear: China would engineer world peace, would be a leader of global development, and would uphold the international order as its guardian. The pathway for Chinese diplomacy would be to seek communication rather than confrontation, while seeking partnership rather than an alliance, pursuing its independent and peaceful foreign policy, while defending its rightful interests, and dedicating itself to the creation of well-established and balanced arrangements for relations with great powers.[15] As analysed by observers, such a message indicates the advent of a key feature of a new world order, as written by China.

Has China Succeeded in Moulding the New World Order?

The post 1991 world order, where the US emerged as the sole hegemon, or the post 2008 world order, where the US learnt to coexist with a rising China, albeit with a little anxiety, has now given way to a new post-pandemic world order; this change can be linked to the intense competition between the US and China. Before one analyses the changes in the existing world order, and whether China has really succeeded in moulding a new order, some clarifications and answers to some questions are essential.

First, and importantly: is the current world order in decline, with particular reference to the US-led order under threat of revisionism by China? Neither of the two questions can be answered in simple black and white, unless one relates to the general affiliations in the political spectrum. The answer, thus, becomes complex, since the world order is complex. It is, therefore, important to understand what international order is and what it implies, for which one has to turn back to the pages of history.

Gilford John Ikenberry, a professor of international relations at Princeton University in USA, has defined the international order as "the organising rules and institutions of world politics...through which (countries) do business".[16] This definition implies that if a country is to be considered as revisionist, as China is presumed to be doing, it should be deliberately trying to alter these rules, change ideas that underpin order, and that it is doing this across the canvas with the help of other countries, which are willing partners in wanting the change.

The world order, as it exists today, albeit with modifications due to changing circumstances, was created and led by USA and its allies after World War II, and the buzzword was multilateralism. The principles of the 1941 Atlantic Charter in which Franklin D. Roosevelt and Winston Churchill declared their shared commitment to free trade and collective security were more formally included in the Bretton Woods Conference of 1944.[17] But today, who is the revisionist? USA, with President Trump advocating 'America First', leading to undermining collective security and walking out of numerous multilateral agreements and institutions, as aforesaid mentioned, or China?

China too, has violated or rejected shared ideas of institutions, which it has joined; it has not ratified the Comprehensive Test Ban Treaty (CTBT), but neither has USA ratified it! At the same time, China has partially or wholly complied with others, but selectively, because it served its interests in doing so. Its joining the UN Convention on the Law of the Sea (UNCLOS) was to serve its own interests. Its embrace of the World Trade Organisation (WTO) has been more total where it has worked to make domestic changes to show to the world that it is in compliance with the WTO system.

Even before the pandemic became a notable disruptor of the global order, it was quite apparent that global values were undergoing metamorphosis. Contrasting aspects influenced the need to change the value-chain, not the least being the inconsistent behaviour of USA in the past few years, which has witnessed deliberate distortion of facts by the administration and the downfall of American absolute power that, as it is, had been on crutches for almost a decade. USA has, almost single-handedly, with its policies in Syria, Algeria, Iran and other flashpoints, widened the arc of instability from North Africa to West Asia and Central Asia, apparently with no consideration for the consequences; the values that it once represented have gradually become more and more unappealing to a majority of the nations. The changing world values are not likely to be aligned with the values that America once cherished.

China's concealing the gravity of the pandemic in the early days of the outbreak, roused world opinion against it; this opaqueness restricted other nations' efforts to contain the spread, which led to high levels of mistrust and antagonism against China in all spheres, further causing attrition to its trustworthiness. Even though China moved on from being chided for its indiscretions, to being complimented for its efficient handling of the pandemic and helping other nations with medical aid, it is implausible to even imagine that there would be consensus any time soon to accept its global leadership.

USA and China are the world's two largest powers, with USA as a status quo power and China as a rising power, and both preferring to be called superpowers. It is basic international relations theory that there has to be friction between two such powers; it is so even between these two countries too, with neither being agreeable to each other, yet compelled to do business with each other! USA argues that China is a beneficiary of the rules-based, liberal, international order, which has helped it become what it is today, namely, a major global power. It was a belief in the West, now belied by China's behaviour, that as China prospered, it would become less autocratic and turn into a more open society. However, instead of seeking to adopt this order, it has walked down a dark path, become more autocratic, wherein its own people have been the first victims, and now it has the rest of the world in its crosshairs. The uncharted territory that US-China frictions will take the rest of the nations through can be compared to coping with parallel universes that may have existed earlier too, more so during the Cold War, but not with the interdependence of the globalised era of today. As a result, divergent choices and competing alternatives in many domains such as technology, commerce and finance, will continue to rest on shared foundations!

It can be said, therefore, that nations that are expected to embrace the current world order, may want to revise certain aspects to turn them beneficial to themselves, while nations that are not expected to do so, may buy into the order, especially when their own interests are at an advantage. The determinants that will contribute to shaping the new world order—exacerbated by the pandemic—will be geopolitical and economic. The apparent end of Pax Americana and the changed outlook towards multilateralism and globalisation demonstrate that these paradigms are not permanent in nature, and, hence, these structures will be reorganised to suit the order of the day. It may also be concluded that the builder of the existing world order, USA in this case, will promote the principles of its own creation in each and every issue. It needs to be remembered that since creating and propping up the norms of the world order is dependent on a concert of countries, it leaves room for the most influential nations to manoeuvre the behaviour of the recalcitrant others, and not necessarily the most powerful.

Concluding Thoughts

Recent years have brought deeply disturbing developments around the globe. As Robert Kagan writes in his book, "In the face of such disarray, a worst possible response based on a misreading of the world, American sentiment seems to be leaning increasingly toward withdrawal and looking inwards."[18] A Russian dictator, would-be European or African dictators, and a Chinese leader, although elected, but who wields total power, all have a commonality of a vision, of changing the world, based on the model of their respective nations. The Western nations once believed that economic successes in autocratic societies would eventually lead to political liberalisation; it is now seen how autocracies practise state-capitalism, in consonance with authoritarian governance; geoeconomics, which had replaced geopolitics, is once again being replaced by geopolitics; the nation-state, once thought of as obsolete in a world of globalisation and inter-connectivity, is also returning in the emerging nationalism and protectionism.

The walking out of USA from the Joint Comprehensive Plan of Action (JCPOA), generally known as the Iran Nuclear Agreement, created serious geopolitical repercussions, some direct in nature, while others more as collateral. The unilateral withdrawal of USA and its subsequent imposition of sanctions on Iran, or any other country dealing with Iran, has not been taken too kindly by its allies, only because of global interdependence. USA's withdrawal from the Paris Accord on Climate, the Trans-Pacific Partnership, and other agreements, and its 'couldn't care less' attitude towards international institutions, has soured relations with its allies, and with other major powers, to become more of a 'give and take' relationship; such actions by the largest existing power have been the primary cause of the undoing of the post-World War II world order.

Once the world recovers from the pandemic—as and when it recovers—new coalitions could emerge, while some earlier ones could become redundant, and may also disappear totally. As the world order metamorphoses and the new world order takes time to establish itself, a stable and judicious approach by all major players, supporting an efficient multilateral order, would be the demand. As events unfold, and unnoticed events appear on the horizon, the competition for global leadership in the 21st century may spring surprising changes that nobody had foreseen.

Notes

1. As quoted in "The New World Disorder", in the 'Leaders' section in *The Economist*, June 18, 2020.
2. Air Mshl Dhiraj Kukreja, "A New World Order—Is it in the Offing", *Air Power—the Journal of Air Power and Space Studies*, Centre for Air Power Studies, Vol. 13, No 4, Winter 2018 (October-December).
3. Ibid.
4. Archived copy of President HW Bush's speech before a Joint Session of Congress on September 11, 1990, available on http://millercenter.org/president/bush/speeches/speech-3425, accessed on September 1, 2018.
5. Ibid.
6. David Hoffman, "Summit Decision Signals Superpower Cooperation", *Washington Post*, September 2, 1990, accessed on September 3, 2018.
7. Christianity Expert, "Henry Kissinger", accessed on September 3, 2018.
8. Archived copy of Prime Minister Tony Blair's speech at the Lord Mayor's Banquet on November 12, 2001, available on https://web.archive.org/web/20090121063703/http://www.number10.gov.uk/Page1661, accessed on September 3, 2018.
9. Thomas Wright, "Stretching the International Order to its Breaking Point", Order from Chaos, April 6, 2020, Brookings Institute, originally in The Atlantic, https://www.brookings.edu/blog/order-from-chaos/2020/04/06/stretching-the-international-order-to-its-breaking-point/?utm_campaign=Foreign%20Policy&utm_source=hs_email&utm_medium=email&utm_content=86138707, accessed on April 17, 2020.

10. Archived copy of Iranian President Mahmoud Ahmedinejad's interview with IRIB, February 17, 2009, https://web.archive.org/web/20090219124613/http://www. presstv.ir/detail.aspx?id=85972&sectionid=351020101, accessed on September 3, 2018.

11. Adam Tooze, "Crashed: How a Decade of Financial Crises Changed the World", Audiobook, available on www.amazon.com.

12. Ibid.

13. Simon Tisdall, "Munich Conference: Three Dangerous Superpowers—and We're Stuck in the Middle", https://www.theguardian.com/commentisfree/2017/feb/19/ munich-security-conference-nato-trump-russia-china-superpowers-europe-pig- in-middle, accessed on September 22, 2018.

14. Xi Jinping, "Secure a Decisive Victory in Building a Moderately Prosperous Society in All Respects and Strive for the Great Success of Socialism with Chinese Characteristics for a New Era," Speech delivered at the 19th National Congress of the Communist Party of China, http://www.xinhuanet.com/english/download/Xi_ Jinping's_report_at_19th_CPC_National_Congress.pdf, accessed on September 23, 2018.

15. Kukreja, n. 2.

16. Manjari C Miller, "Who's Undermining the Global Order", *Hindustan Times*, August 12, 2020.

17. Ibid.

18. Robert Kagan, *The Jungle Grows Back: America and the Imperilled World* (New York: Penguin Random House LLC, 2018).

7. China: Beyond 2021

The Chinese Communist Party

The Chinese Communist Party (CCP) celebrated its centenary on July 1, 2021. With the celebrations, the CCP has shown itself to the world not only as the most successful Communist Party, but also the most successful authoritarian regime in the world—one country, one party—to the extent that China and the CCP are sometimes considered synonymous! In its rule over China for 72 years, it has 'presided' over one of the most astonishing socio-economic transformations ever witnessed in any country. The Chinese leadership is now looking forward to another centenary celebration in 2049, that of the founding of the People's Republic of China (PRC).

The CCP, today, has membership of over 90 million, and yet, despite its common ideology, it means differently to different people. The variations in its recognition are also the main cause of its success. The CCP has proven itself by relying not just on coercion, but also on co-option, and, in the process, shown itself to be ideologically flexible, a contradiction for the world's Communist Parties, which generally follow a strict and narrow path, as dictated by their doctrine. The success story of the CCP is also due to its capacity to blend the many interpretations of Marxist ideology with the modernisation drive, without transforming the core structure, hence, overcoming the many challenges that posed a danger to social stability. The country promotes a classless structure, while simultaneously overseeing and coping with the growth of huge inequality and capitalism in the society. The interests of the urban middle class are at variance with the interests of the peasants and the workers who migrate from the rural areas; China has the largest number of internet users—989 million by the end of 2020—with four companies providing 44 per cent of the global e-commerce[1].

These significant figures are despite stern and unyielding digital censorship, achieved through widespread scrutiny!

Over the years, the CCP has weathered many a storm and proved doomsday prophets wrong about its downfall. Importantly, the main tool employed by the CCP has been to experiment with changes at the local levels, prior to implementing changes at the national level. Deng Xiaoping eloquently termed this practice as "crossing the river by feeling the stones".[2] Mao's policies of the Great Leap Forward and the Cultural Revolution during the 1950s to the 1970s, were, hence, changed for hard-nosed solutions that worked to undo the damage to the country and the society. Factors that influenced these changes were many, but mainly included censorship and purges—practices that have been followed thereafter by the leadership to keep the masses informed and misinformed! Co-option of the urban middle class by dangling the carrot of improved living standards, at par with the Western nations, with high-end technological innovations and world-class infrastructure, lured the society to follow the CCP and its leadership, which otherwise could have faced opposition to the purges and censorship.

Deng Xiaoping, during his tenure at the helm of the CCP and the nation, immediately after the draconian era of Mao, had initiated an era of reforms with a long-sighted view to get China where it is now. His aim was to ensure stability and orderliness in the nation from the chaos of the preceding years, through an initiative to separate the Party from governance and revive the faith of the people in Communism, and, thus, in the Party. He launched economic reforms, established diplomatic relations with USA, and reintroduced many policies that had been discontinued during the Mao era, by opening the country to foreign investment and technology, thus, leading China away from a planned economy and outdated Maoist ideologies. The process of transformation, as begun by Deng, with a few tweaks here and there, continued through the period up to 2012, when Xi Jinping took over the reins.

Xi Jinping has been of the opinion that the people, especially the cadre of the CCP, had been drifting away from the ideology which provided the foundation for the formation of the CCP and the nation. He, therefore, sought to resuscitate official pedagogy by bringing back the ritual of narrations of the Communist classics by the CCP members, and, hence, reviving the belief of the people in Communism. While Deng wanted to separate the Party from the government, Xi Jinping has blended the two by putting the Party firmly in charge. To safeguard this, he has not hesitated to revert to some practices of the Mao era, when ordinary members and students served as the eyes and ears of the CCP in neighbourhoods, places of work, and educational institutions; in Xinjiang, Party committees have been tasked to build detention centres, where more than a million Uighur Muslims are detained, supposedly for re-education. The judiciary has become subservient to the Party, where secretaries, and not a judicial panel or a court has the final say on the arrest or release of a person. With capitalism on the rise, the CCP has managed to rein in private entrepreneurs with regulatory crackdowns, initiation of criminal proceedings, and even confiscation of wealth. The Alibaba Group holding, the e-commerce juggernaut, was the first to be checked for alleged abuse of its monopoly power, followed by Tencent, the technology giant; the CCP feared that these companies had grown so big that they could stray from the Party ideology and control. It is ironical that the restrictive trade practices by the Chinese government on overseas companies had earlier helped them to become the behemoths that they are. "The government has no intention of completely stripping Tencent and Alibaba of their power … the Communist Party just wants them to expand operations within the range of its control" opines Minoru Nogimori, senior economist at the Japan Research Institute.[3]

Strategic and political commentators from the Western nations have predicted many a time over the past the dissolution of the CCP or the transformation of China from a single-party state to a democracy. These hopeful thoughts surfaced at regular intervals: the opening of the economy in the 1980s, or after the massacre at the Tiananmen Square in 1989, or with the outbreak of sporadic unrest in Hong Kong after it was handed over by Britain in 1997. However, the centenary celebrations have shown that this is unlikely to happen in the near future, despite challenges, both internal and external. The spread of the Covid virus within the country had caused discontent to a certain extent, but the country's propaganda machine suppressed the figures for the local populace and the world. Coupled with domestic propaganda, the wolf-warrior diplomats have been working overtime to counter comments in the international media. Apart from the pandemic, China has had to keep its powder dry to cope with USA as an adversary, rather than just a trade and investment partner, as it has been thus far. While the answer on the horizon may be hazy, what is clear is that Xi Jinping, with his extended tenure as Party general secretary and the president of the country, will have to play his cards well to keep the Chinese people and the Party cadre, satisfied.

Xi Jinping—2012-2021...?

It was in November 2012, during the 18th National Congress that Xi Jinping was elected as the general secretary of the CCP and simultaneously appointed as the chairman of the CMC, followed by his election as the president of China in March 2013. Having assumed the posts, he was considered as the 'paramount leader', and began his actions to consolidate his power. His announcements concerning his plan of action to run the country included purging the CCP of corruption, and restoring China to its rightful place in the international order—a rejuvenation of the nation. (For a detailed account, read Chapter 5, China: Xi Jinping at the Helm)

To achieve his goals, Xi Jinping needed to strengthen his authority over the cadres of the Party for which he needed control over all important committees and commissions; he ensured this, with some deft political manoeuvring, through the anti-corruption campaign, which was also used to purge his political rivals and place his own coterie in positions of power. Setting aside of the principle of collective leadership, as was advocated by Deng Xiaoping, made Xi Jinping, already the paramount leader, the most powerful too, after Mao Zedong. Further political reforms were announced during the 19th Party Congress wherein those either too old, or of doubtful loyalty or integrity, or placed in important commissions by earlier leaders, were removed. Xi Jinping had, thus, established himself firmly, to amend the Constitution during the National People's Congress in 2018, to abolish the presidential term limits by 2,958 votes in favour, two opposing and three abstaining votes.[4] His actions were clearly indicative of his aspiration to continue in power beyond October 2022, when the 20th National Congress would be convened to elect a new general secretary.

Xi Jinping's actions to eradicate any opposition to him and his policies have generated discontent, but it has been suppressed since he has a firm hold over the CCP, the military as well as the political institutions. Rumours do go around in Beijing and other provincial capitals that the seemingly invincible leader is in trouble, especially when China continues to be in a dogged trade war with USA, with a see-saw economy and public health scandals that involve not only the handling of the pandemic, but also earlier ones regarding children being inoculated with sub-standard vaccines and others![5]

While critics and activists have closed-door debates, and rumours do thrive, they lack credibility. To quell the rumours and criticism on social media and elsewhere, the state-run propaganda machine manages public opinion, be it about the vaccines, the abolition of the presidential term limit or the most recent handling of the Covid pandemic. *The Global Times*, in an editorial in August 2018, claimed, "If there is no management of public opinion, it can fester and lead the country to chaos ... We must have the ability to prevent destructive elements from spreading online."[6] Such inserts in the media, along with strict censorship, are indications of the draconian measures adopted by the present regime in China to ensure that Xi Jinping continues to remain in full control.

Xi Jinping believes in absolute power, not just for himself, but also for the CCP. While addressing the 19th Congress of the CCP in October 2017, he told the audience, "The Party controls all".[7] If Deng Xiaoping was instrumental in launching reforms to distance the Party from the government, Xi Jinping has done otherwise and has brought the Party back into all facets of politics and society. Almost all the principal aspects of Deng's reforms have been rolled back and Xi is now commonly portrayed as *zhuxi* (chairman), *lingxiu* (leader), *hexin* (core), and even *da duoshou* (great helmsman), terms reminiscent of the Mao era.[8]

The Party's Propaganda Department, along with the state-run media, has been working overtime to promote Xi Jinping's image as a lovable leader, who has not forgotten his roots. Stories of unselfish service during his youth that was spent in a small village during the Cultural Revolution, and after his becoming president, standing in a queue in a restaurant, have been spread to portray him as a common man; articles in the media refer to him as Xi Dada—translated as 'Uncle Xi' or 'Big Daddy Xi', and a video, titled 'Xi Dada loves Peng Mama' which highlights his relationship with his wife, Peng Liyuan, is viewed widely![9]

The year 2020 is considered to be an important milestone in the tenure of Xi Jinping. The crisis of the pandemic that supposedly started from the city of Wuhan, was expected to write off Xi Jinping's authority within the country and his ambition to gain world leadership. Instead, he has emerged stronger than before, both within the country and globally, with many nations looking towards China for assistance in controlling the spread of the deadly virus. Very few analysts and critics could have even foreseen such a turn of events! As the year progressed, China's economy rebounded, while the world economy steadily headed southwards. 2020 was also the year that Xi had promised in 2015, by which extreme poverty would be eradicated and a 'moderately prosperous society' built in the country; in February 2021, amidst much fanfare, the announcement of having eliminated extreme poverty and achieved the 'human miracle', one month in advance of the self-imposed deadline, was made in Beijing.[10] Notwithstanding the critics and sceptics, by the end of 2020, Xi Jinping had once again re-established himself and silenced the dissidents in preparation for November 2022, when he comes up for re-election or relinquishing of his post.

The annual meeting of China's national legislature, normally referred to as the National People's Congress (NPC), and generally held in the month of March, was postponed for the first time in decades, as the country grappled with the fast-spreading Covid virus pandemic; the meeting, however, was held in the month of May 2020, after an announcement to that effect in April. The announcement was, essentially, for the consumption of the general public and the international community that China had successfully controlled the spread of the virus.

In March 2021, when the candidates gathered for the traditional NPC and the Chinese People's Political Consultative Conference (CPPCC)— colloquially known as the Two Sessions—it was expected that only the 14th Five-Year Plan would be on the agenda for approval. However, in addition, there was also another unusual, far-sighted plan for development by 2035 that was included for discussion and was, then, approved. To the China-watchers in the Western nations, the people of China, and other leaders of the Politburo, this was another indication of Xi Jinping's intention to extend his tenure beyond 2022! First, there was the chest-thumping announcement in February 2021 of the eradication of extreme poverty in the country, and then the conduct of the annual NPC in March 2021; this was to tell the world that it was business as usual, and that China had full control to stop the spread of the pandemic.

With the passing of the far-sighted development plan up to 2035, the year 2021, hence, is of great significance in Xi's presidency and a near confirmation of his continuation in office beyond 2022. The Chinese state-run media too, pitched in by singing praises of achievements, not of institutions or of other leaders, but only of Xi Jinping, as the sole person, who had the people's interest foremost in his mind and the "broad vision and extraordinary courage of a Marxist politician and strategist".[11] With such a build-up to his campaign for the third term, the CCP propaganda, and suppression of dissent, if any, could there be any doubts in anyone's mind about who would be the successor to Xi Jinping? Steven Tsang, director of the China Institute of the School of Oriental and African Studies, at London, had commented in March 2021 itself, well before the 'selection' process of November 2022, "We know exactly who the successor to Xi Jinping is, it's even clearer than ever.... Xi Jinping."[12] Crystal-ball gazing is a very difficult task, more so in a country like China, which is shrouded in secrecy. Nevertheless, with the turn of events of 2020-2021, even the most die-hard sceptics agreed that Xi Jinping would continue at the helm for a third term. One has only to wait and watch till November 2022!

China's Ambitions: The Lion Awakens[13]

If Xi Jinping has indicated his intentions to continue as general secretary and president till 2035, what does he hope to achieve for China in the years until 2035, when he himself, would be about 82 years old? China today, in the world of the 21st century, claims to be a global power and does not like being referred to as a rising or an emerging or a big regional power, and, hence, demands acceptance as such; with the status of being a global power, come certain rights and privileges, for which, too, China seeks acceptance. It wants to be heard and consulted in regional and international issues with a reasonably correct logic: China is an established economic and military power of the 21st century, and, hence, demands the right to stand along USA to shape the international order.

Xi Jinping, as early as 2013, had formulated a strategy for China for its recognition as a major power; the main theme of the strategy being that both USA and China recognise each other as a major power in the global system, leading to mutually beneficial cooperation.[14] This was China's perspective; however, the American perspective was divergent. USA wanted an unambiguous understanding from China that even if China's perspective of a major country model was accepted, it would not mean an acknowledgement by it of Chinese core national interests, which included its trade practices and territorial ambitions in the South China Sea (SCS). While efforts were made by President Obama in his two tenures in the White House, through meetings with President Hu Jintao and later with President Xi Jinping, three major issues continued as pin-pricks: which of the two nations—USA and China—would write the rules of the global economy; accusations by USA on Chinese cyber activities and illegal interventions—espionage and hacking; Chinese activities of land reclamation in the SCS, military activities on artificial islands, thus, created, and claims on the Exclusive Economic Zones (EEZ) of the littoral nations.[15] Such an assessment by USA of its relations with China, showed that it considered China as an unequal power, and sharing power between unequal nations was just not an option for it. China, therefore, continued, and will continue, in its efforts for power projection, not to be discouraged by any world event or any world leader or any changes in the ever-evolving geopolitical situation.

The Chinese approach to the world is governed by one critical factor above all else: its perception of relative power in relation to USA. The guiding thread in Xi's strategy is the immense continuity in this approach to the world; at the hub of this continuity is the steadfast focus on national rejuvenation that would enable China to be at the peak of the global order. Xi Jinping, as also his predecessors, have spoken of rejuvenation from the day they assumed power; however, it has been only Xi Jinping, who has acted vigorously on it and locked horns with the other 'sole' power, USA.

As narrated earlier, Xi Jinping articulated a strategy to equate China with USA in 2013. However, China is working to achieve total supremacy by 2049, the centenary of the establishment of the People's Republic of China (PRC), with the CCP still strong and growing after its own centenary in 2021. Sceptics, across the world and especially in the US, repeatedly voice their doubts on China continuing its chosen path with a strategy, if any. Rush Doshi, in his book, *The Long Game: China's Grand Strategy to Displace American Order*, describes it succinctly.[16] Some of the sceptics quoted in Doshi's book feel that "China is yet to formulate a true grand strategy"[17], and even questioning its will to do so. In contrast, there is the group of believers, who, while quoting examples of Chinese moves to dismantle US influence and regional alliances, have not been able to put forth any convincing arguments for their perspective.[18] Even the arguments placed by Michael Pillsbury, an adviser to the highest echelons in the American government for many years, in his book, *The Hundred-Year Marathon: China's Secret Strategy to Replace America as the Global Superpower*, have been trashed. The thesis of his book reads: "Once ensconced in its new position of power, China will set up a world order that will be fair to China, a world without American global supremacy, and revise the US-dominated economic and geopolitical world order founded at Bretton Woods and San Francisco at the end of World War II. These 'frightening plans' have been concealed from a gullible United States, which in its misreading of the PRC's intentions, has aided its drive for global control through technology transfers, technical assistance, and economic aid."[19] This thesis, after due study, has been disparaged in the cited piece.

While sceptics may have discounted China's strategy, China does have its ambitions and the leaders, ever since Mao, have been methodically working towards achieving those ambitions. If Mao Zedong is remembered as the leader who proclaimed the PRC in 1949, and thereafter for his Great Leap Forward and the Cultural Revolution, both of which had disastrous results with an unprecedented famine due to the former and widespread subjugation and violence due to the latter, he is also remembered for permeating the Party cadre and government machinery with a revolutionary sentiment. Applauded for reinstilling nationalism amongst the people after winning the civil war against the Kuomintang (KMT)—a nationalist party itself— Mao was considered as the most powerful, yet controversial leader thus far (Xi Jinping is now considered as the most powerful and controversial leader, after Mao); major industrial reforms were initiated and the status of women improved in his time, but with intense suffering and sociopolitical beliefs.

The era after Mao's death witnessed the rise of 'second-generation' leaders of the CCP. Deng Xiaoping is credited for initiating the process of reforms, much different from what Mao had professed; the focus of Deng's reforms encompassed agriculture, industry, science and technology, and defence. If Deng is considered as the architect of modern China, critics deride him for the drastic military-crackdown during the students' protests at Tiananmen Square in 1989. Having assumed the leadership after a brief, but intense, power struggle with Mao's widow, Deng, with an aim for a smooth transition of power, fixed a tenure of two terms for the presidency.

After Deng, Jiang Zemin took over the reins of the country. Although he continued with many of the policies of his predecessor, Jiang introduced the modalities of 'collective leadership', with an aim to avoid the growth of a personality cult. The continuation of earlier policies and reforms saw an era of significant economic growth in China. Jiang handed over the baton to Hu Jintao, considered a 'fourth generation' leader. Hu professed two main ideological concepts for China: scientific development and a balanced, congruent, and harmonious society. China's economic and military growth, called 'peaceful' by its leaders, continued, with the rest of the world watching it warily, for it was during this time that China began its overt display of assertiveness in the region, especially in the SCS. The economic prosperity, however, did not lead to any ideological changes in the CCP, or any major political reforms.

As can be interpreted from the brief above, each leader contributed towards the growth of China, in his own way. The ambition, hence, can be summarised thus: to make China a great nation, once again. China stepped into the 21st century, not as a growing regional power, but as a world power, wanting to claim all the rights and privileges that such a status confers. While in the past, China, through its scholars and officials, referred to itself as an emerging or a regional power, it now called itself as a 'big power'—*zhongguo shi yige daguo*.[20] Xi Jinping, even as the vice-president, had announced this, during a visit to USA in early 2012, when he proposed to define the relationship between USA and China as one among major countries,[21] and as aforementioned, again in 2013, when he had been declared president.

China Beyond 2021: Crystal-ball Gazing

Crystal-ball predictions are very difficult to make, and, at times, turn out to be incorrect. Xi Jinping, on taking over as general secretary of the CCP and, subsequently, as the president of the country, made the task of foretelling the future of China, somewhat easier. He disclosed his 'Chinese Dream' (*Zhong Meng*), which signifies a "powerful and prosperous" China as a "great modern socialist country" by the mid-21st century,[22] which perchance happens to coincide with the centenary of the proclamation of the PRC in 2049! Will Xi Jinping still be around to witness the realisation of his Chinese Dream? The crystal-ball does not give a clear picture!

During the nine years of his rule, leading to 2021, Xi Jinping has ensured the continued growth of China through the initiation of certain measures. On the geoeconomic route, China granted loans on easy terms, luring the unaware nations into a debt-trap, when they could not repay the amounts, also called the practise of 'cheque-book diplomacy'. The Belt and Road Initiative (BRI) in developing nations, both within and out of the region, and some EU nations too, has been used, fairly extensively, to tempt the governments to join what China calls the path to common prosperity. On the geopolitical front, he strengthened his hold over the newly-modernised military to venture strongly into the SCS, the East China Sea, and Eastern Ladakh in India, and also to threaten Taiwan. To ensure the stability and continuity of his rule, on the domestic front, he removed the two-term restrictions on the presidency, purged his political rivals under the pretext of an anti-corruption drive, and inducted his thoughts on "New Era Socialism with Chinese Characteristics" in the Constitution of the CCP (this is also now a part of the curriculum in China's schools and colleges); by getting students to read and understand his thoughts, the CCP wants them to imbibe them into their thinking and actions in all walks of life, while developing love and loyalty for the Party, socialism and the country.[23]

The route that China is following to reclaim its greatness on the global stage, while offering opportunities, has greater potential for conflict, the areas being the SCS, challenging the sovereignty of Taiwan and trade relations with USA and other nations. As China continues with its assertive behaviour, nations across the world wonder how to influence China's illiberal attitude to conform it with their liberal world order. The years 2020 and 2021 have seen China becoming more repressive in Hong Kong and in its western region of Xinjiang, while the world copes with the Covid virus-induced pandemic. In a pandemic-induced global recession, the Chinese economy has reportedly grown initially at a whopping 18 per cent; forecasts indicate that in the coming years, China will account for 30 per cent of global economic growth.[24] In the years ahead, as China continues to grow in its own way, it is doubtful if any nation will initiate any major steps against it. To successfully counter the challenges posed by the Chinese growth, nations have to first understand the complexity of the challenges, the threats they pose to their respective economic and national security, and then develop a *modus operandi*, either singularly or multilaterally.

The centenary celebrations of the CCP, on July 1, 2021, proved many assessments wrong; not only has the Party survived this long, it has survived far longer than it was expected to, and has come out far stronger than what was predicted. When in 1991, the Soviet Union imploded, many 'thinkers' thought that China, with its CCP, would be next; how wrong they were! China, with its one-party rule, has been successful due to three reasons: ruthlessness, ideological agility, and economic growth.

Xi Jinping and his band of leaders have shown no remorse whatsoever, about the ruthless crushing of the students' protests in Tiananmen Square in 1989. Although, a little hesitant, initially, Deng Xiaoping used brutal and lethal power against a peaceful protest, which forced the protesters, and the rest of the nation into submission. The second reason for the longevity of the CCP is the quick changeover from Mao's ideology to adopting Deng's proposals for a market-economy. Staunch Maoist-believers were sidelined, many state-owned companies were closed down, a large number of workers were left jobless, but China's economy showed a boom, leading to an enthusiastic adoption of capitalism. Under Xi Jinping now, the CCP has reverted its focus to 'orthodox ideology'; even mild dissent is not tolerated. The contribution of Mao Zedong is once again lauded, but with no mention of the horrors of the famine and the Cultural Revolution; deviant and corrupt officials in the bureaucracy, military, and police have been removed and the network of the Party cadre has been injected into private companies, large and small, to spy and report on them.

Lastly, China, despite its growing corruption over the years, did not have its leaders turn into outright kleptocrats; the people tended to overlook some corruption, even as their standard of living was improving too. The gains, may not have been generous, but, whatever little, they were appreciated by the people.[25]

The future does not look bleak for China and Xi Jinping. It is expected that Xi Jinping will continue his hold over the Party, and through it, over all the important institutions. Dissent and disagreements, as and when they arise, will continue to be crushed through the vast network of spies and through support from technology. Rural and urban China has its roads and streets fitted with numerous cameras with facial-recognition software; social media accounts are closely monitored and censored, whenever any dissension appears; citizens, who are perceived to be irritants, are either persecuted or lose their jobs, or just simply disappear. In other words, repression is prevalent and will continue to prevail.

Final Words

Notwithstanding the chaos created by the COVID-19 pandemic, Xi's tenuous hold over China does not seem to be facing any major challenges. The 19th Party Congress has consolidated his position, and, hence, the mandate for change within the country has only strengthened. Xi Jinping's thoughts have been included, not only in the Constitution, but also in the curriculum; this would ensure that the CCP members and the students of all ages understand the nuances of socialism and develop loyalty towards the Party. Xi Jinping's speech from the balcony of Tiananmen Gate, dressed in a Mao suit, on the occasion of the Party's 100-year celebrations, was delivered with a sense of victory and applauded by the audience; highlighting the Party's role in making China a globally important nation, Xi Jinping stoked nationalism in the people, stating that "the Chinese people will absolutely not allow any foreign force to bully, oppress or enslave us and anyone who attempts to do so will face broken heads and bloodshed in front of the iron Great Wall of the 1.4 billion Chinese people".[26]

A comparative study of the contemporary world may not be in favour of China. Despite some rollback of democratic norms in certain parts of the world, all major economies continue with democratic governance, except

China. The strategic course of Xi Jinping's leadership is quite evident—to make a world order based on China's political and economic trends! China (Xi Jinping) is convinced, more so after the first Gulf War and the collapse of the Soviet Union, that it is USA that poses the biggest challenge to it—ideologically, militarily, economically, and geopolitically—and, hence, the need to blunt the challenge. China, initially, adopted Deng Xiaoping's 'hide and bide' strategy, but after the global financial crisis of 2007-2009, it was sure in its mind that the American influence was waning, and, as the leadership changed hands, so did China's policies. It was Xi Jinping who finally took it upon himself to discard Deng's policy and participate more actively in global affairs. Militarily, it began strengthening its armed forces, especially the navy and air force; geographically it spread its tentacles through the military; economically, it initiated the Belt and Road Initiative (BRI); diplomatically, it started using its soft power by creating cultural institutions abroad and also started the aggressive trend of 'wolf-warrior' diplomacy. Donald Trump's election followed by his 'America first' policies and then his defeat after just one term, the totally mismanaged response to tackle the pandemic in the Western world in 2019-2020, and the bungled withdrawal of the US and NATO troops from Afghanistan in August 2021, are just some of the other events that have furthered China's opinion that the West is in a decline, probably irreversible. Xi Jinping sees this as a 'once in a life-time opportunity' for China to attain global dominance, completing the changeover in the world order by 2049.

Some Western sceptics, among the numerous scholars, may still have their doubts, stating that there is no conclusive evidence in China's growth pattern that can help it attain the apex position as the sole super-power in the near future, and would thence call for a strong American response. Nevertheless, it is an accepted fact that China today is not just the single party-state of yesterday, but has transformed into an authoritarian technocracy, wanting to replicate its 'China model' across the world.

Many questions arise. Does China have the capability to achieve its ambitions of placing itself in a regional and global order? Can China project its leadership in regional and international political and economic institutions to propagate its autocratic norms? Can the PLA, with its navy and air force show its presence all over the world with its growing armada of aircraft carriers and fleets of new advanced fighter aircraft by establishing overseas bases? Can the waves of internal dissent in China be supressed before they become a tsunami?

Xi Jinping is seeking greatness for China; this has been oft-repeated in his speeches when he calls for rejuvenation of the great Chinese nation. Thus far, his efforts do not seem to have shown much success, although China claims to have developed a military to challenge USA (as per its own claims) and is the world's second-largest economy. The BRI is not progressing as per Xi Jinping's plans, having been hampered by the pandemic, and many nations seeing through the mala fide intentions of China's debt diplomacy. The world population does not seem to have faith in China's political system, cultural values and social norms, and is rejecting the views put forth in the many Confucian Institutes—a failure for Xi Jinping's soft power diplomacy. The findings of a new Pew Research Centre survey conducted between February 1-May 26, 2021 in 17 advanced economies, show that not many are sure of Xi Jinping doing the right thing in world affairs, with the negative appraisal being at historic lows in most countries/places. While the same report does show an acceptance of China's handling of the pandemic in 2021, as better than the previous year, most people in nations across Europe, North America, and the Asia-Pacific feel that China does not respect the individual liberties of its own people.[27] Internally, as aforementioned, Xi Jinping has cracked down on private enterprises, which were once considered as the strength of the Chinese economy. The most dangerous threat that Xi Jinping faces, or is likely to face after 2022, will, probably be, not from the masses, but from within the cadres of the CCP. Notwithstanding all his efforts, and the grand centenary celebrations of the CCP, it suffers from factionalism, disloyalty, and ideological ennui. The rivals to Xi Jinping may have been jailed, but the succession that is due in 2022, or later, could be, in all probability, the decisive moment.

Globally too, China has not shown workable solutions, except where its own interests are at stake and can be easily advanced, only in nations where China is involved in infrastructure and economic development through the BRI or security cooperation to curtail terrorist attacks through the Shanghai

Cooperation Organisation (SCO). It has not been able to control (willingly?) North Korea's nuclear proliferation, or take the lead in the vacuum created by Donald Trump's 'America First' policies. Nevertheless, with Xi Jinping, at the helm, and all set for a third-term in November 2022, China can succeed in the globalised world only if it does not shut its doors to new ideas and influences from the outside.

An attempt has been made to answer the aforementioned questions and more that may arise in the minds of the reader, however, only time can tell if China has the potential.

Even as the years pass, and some answers emerge, China will continue to remain what it is now—an enigma!

Notes

1. Pallavi Aiyar, "Coercion and Cooption: Twin Secrets to CCP's Longevity," *Times of India* (ToI), July 4, 2021.

2. Ibid.

3. Hiroshi Murayama, "China's Tech Crackdown Widens to Tencent from Alibaba", August 8, 2021, https://asia.nikkei.com/Business/China-tech, accessed on August 9, 2021.

4. James Doubek, "China Removes Presidential Term Limits, Enabling Xi Jinping to Rule Indefinitely" Nevada Public Radio (knpr.org) March 11, 2018, accessed on March 1, 2021.

5. Lily Kuo, "They are Devils: China's Parents Demand Answers over Vaccine Scandal", *The Guardian*, July 25, 2018, accessed on August 8, 2021.

6. Ibid.

7. David Shambaugh, "China Under Xi Jinping", East Asia Forum, November 19 2018, https://www.eastasiaforum.org/2018/11/19/china-under-xi-jinping/, accessed on June 14, 2021.

8. Ibid.

9. Elizabeth C. Economy, *The Third Revolution* (Oxford University Press, 2018), p. 24.

10. "Xi Jinping Declares China Created 'Human Miracle' of Eliminating Extreme Poverty", NDTV, https://www.ndtv.com/world-news/president-xi-jinping-declares-china-created-human-miracle-of-eliminating-extreme-poverty-2378250, accessed on June 14, 2021.

11. Ben Westcott, "An Analysis: With no Successor in Sight, Xi Jinping Heads to Major Party Meeting with More Power Than Ever", March 5, 2021, https://edition.cnn.com/2021/03/04/asia/xi-jinping-china-npc-successor-intl-hnk/index.html, accessed on March 15, 2021.

12. Ibid.

13. Economy, n. 9, "The Lion Awakens" is the title of Chapter 7 in the quoted book.

14. Ruan Zongze, "A New Model of Major-Country Relations: The New Driving Force Behind China-US Relations", China-US Focus, December 24, 2013, https://www.chinausfocus.com/foreign-policy/a-new-model-of-major-country-relations-the-new-driving-force-behind-china-us-relations, accessed on March 15, 2021.

15. Namrata Goswami, "China-US Relations: Sharing Power is not an Option", IDSA, in Jagannath Panda, ed., *China's Year Book 2015—China's Transition Under Xi Jinping* (Pentagon Press, 2016), available at https://idsa.in/system/files/book/book_china-transition-under-xi-jinping.pdf, accessed on March 20, 2021.

16. Rush Doshi, *The Long Game* (Oxford University Press, July 2021), Excerpts available on The long game: China's grand strategy to displace American order (brookings.edu), accessed on August 7, 2021.

17. Ibid.

18. Ibid.

19. Jude Blanchette, "The Devil is in the Footnotes: On Reading Michael Pillsbury's The Hundred-Year Marathon", 21st Century China Program, School of International Relations and Pacific Studies, The-Hundred-Year-Marathon.docx (ucsd.edu), accessed on August 27, 2021.

20. Economy, n. 9, p. 186.

21. Ibid.

22. Maj Gen GG Dwivedi, "History of the CPC and its Leaders—and President Xi's Ambitious New Long March for China", *The Indian Express*, June 30, 2021, Explained News, *The Indian Express*, accessed on July 2, 2021.

23. "President Xi Jinping's Political Ideology to Become Part of Curriculum in China", *Times of India*, August 25, 2021.

24. "The West Cannot Force China to Read its Interests Differently", Chaguan, *The Economist*, July 2, 2020, accessed on July 3, 2020.

25. "China's Communist Party at 100: The Secret of its Longevity", Leaders, *The Economist*, June 26, 2021, accessed on June 27, 2021.

26. "Communist Party Marks Centenary: Xi Jinping Vows China Will Never be Bullied", *Times of India*, July 2, 2021.

27. Laura Silver, Kat Devlin, Christine Huang, "Large Majorities Say China Does Not Respect the Personal Freedoms of Its People", Report of Pew Research Centre, June 30, 2021, accessed on July 14, 2021.

Index

www.ingramcontent.com/pod-product-compliance
Lightning Source LLC
Chambersburg PA
CBHW020812100426
42814CB00001B/29